D0214891

OXFORD CLASSICAL AND PHILOSOPHICAL MONOGRAPHS

Published under the supervision of a Committee of the Faculty of Literae Humaniores in the University of Oxford

Exits and Entrances in Menander

K. B. FROST

CLARENDON PRESS · OXFORD
1988

Oxford University Press, Walton Street, Oxford OX2 6DP
Oxford New York Toronto
Delhi Bombay Calcutta Madras Karachi
Petaling Jaya Singapore Hong Kong Tokyo
Nairobi Dar es Salaam Cape Town
Melbourne Auckland
and associated companies in
Beirut Berlin Ibadan Nicosia

Oxford is a trade mark of Oxford University Press

Published in the United States
by Oxford University Press, New York

British Library Cataloguing in Publication Data
Frost, K. B.
Exits and entrances in Menander.—
(Oxford classical and philosophical monographs).
1. Menander, 342–292 B.C.—Criticism and interpretation
I. Title
882′.01 PA4247
ISBN 0-19-814723-6

Library of Congress Cataloging in Publication Data
Frost, K. B.
Exits and entrances in Menander.
Modified version of thesis (M.Litt.)—Oxford University, 1984.
Includes index.
1. Menander, of Athens—Technique. 2. Classical drama (Comedy)—History and criticism. 3. Drama—Technique. I. Title.
PA4247.F74 1988 882′.01 87-22026
ISBN 0-19-814723-6

Typeset by Joshua Associates Limited, Oxford
Printed in Great Britain by
Biddles Ltd, Guildford and King's Lynn

Preface

THIS book is a modified version of an Oxford M. Litt. thesis submitted in 1984. In preparing the work for publication I have deleted or severely condensed the sections of the thesis which dealt with Roman Comedy, partly to focus more sharply on the surviving Menander and partly through a privately held scepticism about the value of the 'Latin Menander' to reconstruct anything beyond the most general outline of the Greek originals. However, I have usually tried to indicate further reading for those interested in linking more closely the Latin with the Greek evidence.

Stagecraft in ancient drama has inspired a good number of publications in the last decade, and all the fifth-century dramatists have received some kind of treatment. Perhaps it is because the fragments of Menander were discovered so recently that they have tended to be the preserve of textual critics or social historians, and it was largely through dissatisfaction at the secondary importance afforded to the plays as scripts for production that I was first led to examine the topic of stagecraft in Menander. The user of this book will decide whether I have successfully avoided crossing the thin line between legitimate deduction of action from the text and unsupported flights of fancy.

My postgraduate work was supervised by Mr P. G. McC. Brown of Trinity College, Oxford, who provided every encouragement to my research while restraining some of my wilder speculations; he is not, of course, to be held responsible for any of the views contained in this book. My examiners, Dr D. Bain of Manchester University and Mr J. C. B. Lowe of Bedford College, London provided a number of helpful suggestions. Finally I wish to thank my wife Kathryn for her encouragement during the writing of this work both as a thesis and then for publication. As a small token of thanks I dedicate it to her.

K.B.F.

Oxford
May, 1987

Contents

Bibliography and Symbols

Arnott (1979)	Arnott, W. G., *Menander* (Loeb, vol. i; London).
Austin (1969)	Austin, C., *Menandri* Aspis *et* Samia, i (Berlin).
Austin (1970)	Austin, C., *Menandri* Aspis *et* Samia, ii (Berlin).
Bain (1977)	Bain, D., *Actors and Audience* (Oxford).
Bain (1979)	Bain, D., 'Plautus Vortit Barbare', in D. West and A. Woodman (edd.), *Creative Imitation and Latin Literature* (Cambridge), 17–34.
Bain (1981)	Bain, D., *Masters, Servants and Orders in Greek Tragedy* (Manchester).
Blume (1974)	Blume, H. D., *Menanders* Samia (Darmstadt).
Blundell (1980)	Blundell, J., *Menander and the Monologue* (Göttingen).
CGF	Austin, C., *Comicorum Graecorum Fragmenta in Papyris Reperta* (Berlin and New York, 1973).
Duckworth (1952)	Duckworth, G. E., *The Nature of Roman Comedy* (Princeton).
Flickinger (1936)	Flickinger, R. C., *The Greek Theater and its Drama* (Chicago).
Fraenkel (1912)	Fraenkel, E., *De Media et Nova Comoedia Quaestiones Selectae* (Göttingen).
Fraenkel (1922)	Fraenkel, E., *Plautinisches im Plautus* (Berlin).
Gilula (1979)	Gilula, D., 'Exit Motivations and Actual Exits in Terence', *AJP* 100, 519–30.
Goldberg (1980)	Goldberg, S. M., *The Making of Menander's Comedy* (London).
Gomme (1937)	Gomme, A. W., 'Menander', in *Essays in Greek History and Literature* (Oxford), 249–95.
GS	Gomme, A. W. and Sandbach, F. H., *Menander: A Commentary* (Oxford, 1973).
Gorler (1963)	Gorler, W., ΜΕΝΑΝΔΡΟΥ ΓΝΩΜΑΙ (Berlin).
Handley (1965)	Handley, E. W., *The* Dyskolos *of Menander* (London).
Handley (1970)	Handley, E. W., 'The Conventions of the Comic Stage and their Exploitation by Menander', *Entretiens Hardt* 16, 3–26.
Harms (1914)	Harms, C., *De Introitu Personarum in Euripidis et Novae Comoediae Fabulis* (Göttingen).
Holzberg (1974)	Holzberg, N., *Menander* (Nuremberg).
Jacques (1978)	Jacques, J. M., 'Mouvement des acteurs et conventions

scéniques dans l'acte II du *Bouclier* de Ménandre', *Grazer Beiträge*, 7, 37–56.

Kassel (1965) Kassel, R., *Sicyonius* (Berlin).

Katsouris (1975) Katsouris, A. G., *Tragic Patterns in Menander* (Athens).

Koch (1914) Koch, W., *De Personarum Comicarum Introductione* (Breslau).

Legrand (1910) Legrand, P. E., *Daos: Tableau de la comédie grecque pendant la période dite nouvelle* (Lyons and Paris).

Leo (1908) Leo, F., *Der Monolog in Drama* (Berlin).

Mastronarde (1979) Mastronarde, D. J., *Contact and Discontinuity: Some Conventions of Speech and Action on the Greek Stage* (University of California Publications, Classical Studies, 21; Berkeley and Los Angeles).

Mooney (1914) Mooney, W. W., *The House-door on the Ancient Stage* (Baltimore).

Newiger (1979) Newiger, H. J., 'Drama und Theater', in G. A. Seeck (ed.), *Das griechische Drama* (Darmstadt), 434–63.

Sandbach (1970) Sandbach, F. H., 'Menander's Manipulation of Language for Dramatic Purposes', *Entretiens Hardt* 16, 113–36.

Sandbach (1975) Sandbach, F. H., 'Menander and the Three-Actor Rule', in O. Bingen *et al*. (edd.), *Le Monde grec: Hommages à Claire Préaux* (Brussels), 197–204.

Taplin (1977) Taplin, O., *The Stagecraft of Aeschylus* (Oxford).

Webster (1960) Webster, T. B. L., *Studies in Menander*[2] (Manchester).

Webster (1974) Webster, T. B. L., *An Introduction to Menander* (Manchester).

Wilamowitz (1925) Wilamowitz, U.v., *Das Schiedsgericht* (Berlin).

Note

(?) following a reference indicates that the interpretation of the cited passage is based on conjecture and that further discussion is to be found in the note on the passage in the second part of the volume.

In the description of movements in the second part of the volume [ ] indicates that the movement or action contained within the brackets is conjectural as a result of the fragmentary state of the text.

References in footnotes to A(3), B(1), etc. refer the reader to specific sections of the general discussion in the Introduction.

Abbreviations of journal titles follow the system adopted in *L'Année philologique*.

Introduction

THE original text of Menander is now available in sufficient quantities to enable us to attempt a judgement of his stagecraft in general and his handling of exits and entrances in particular. Scholarly opinion has been favourable, with G. F. Davidson writing in 1932[1] of 'the extreme effectiveness of certain entrances in the fragments of Menander', while more recently Taplin (1977) 67 n. 1 has remarked on 'the intricately realistic motivations in Men. *Dysc.*'.[2] Menander's reputation has certainly profited from comparison with Plautus and Terence: Bain (1977) highlights the frequent absence from his text of explicit indications of the accompanying action, particularly in the form of 'stage-directional' phrases so beloved of the Roman comedians, noting 'the restraint shown by Menander in the use of conventional phrases; in general it may be said that Plautus and to a lesser, but not all that significantly lesser, extent Terence explain far more than Menander ever does, and that the impression they leave is of an almost Homeric delight in certain more or less fixed formulae' (p. 153; cf. 135ff., 177ff.). A close examination of the means by which entrances and exits are managed in the surviving plays can yield instructive examples both to support and illustrate the general approbation afforded to Menander and to highlight the occasional passages which do contain 'conventional' or 'stage-directional' phrases not entirely dissimilar to those common in the Roman comedians.

The following study examines the more complete fragments of Menander with the aim of establishing the various ways in which exits and entrances are managed,[3] and attempts to show how these ways were used both to create certain effects in performance and on occasion to permit dramatic short cuts to be taken. Where relevant the evidence of the Latin adaptations of Menander (Plautus' *Aulularia*,[4]

[1] *HSPh* 43 (1932), 170.

[2] See also Gomme (1937) 254–5.

[3] One major method, the entrance monologue, is excluded from the discussion of entrance technique in the Introduction since the subject has been given ample treatment by Bain (1977) 135–6 and Blundell (1980) *passim*.

[4] No direct evidence for Menandrean authorship of the original, but displaying a striking number of Menandrean features, on which see W. G. Arnott, *Phoenix*, 18 (1964),

Bacchides,[5] *Cistellaria*,[6] and *Stichus*,[7] Terence's *Andria*,[8] *HT*,[9] *Eunuchus*,[10] and *Adelphoe*[11]) is used for comparison or contrast. (This list is not intended to exclude the possibility that other surviving Roman comedies may also derive from Menandrean originals.[12]) In the chapter that follows a brief discussion, intended as an introduction and not a definitive statement, of some dramatic conventions which directly bear on stage movements is followed by a survey of the principal means by which characters are moved on and off the stage. On points of individual detail the reader is referred to the play-by-play analysis in the second part of the book.

A. SOME DRAMATIC CONVENTIONS

A(1) *The Three-actor Rule*

There is no direct evidence that in Greek Comedy of Menander's time a conventional restriction to three speaking actors existed.[13] What evidence there is concerns earlier drama and is largely inconclusive: tragedies of the fifth century are on the whole not inconsistent with such a restriction, but some comedies of Aristophanes cannot be performed without a fourth speaker, while in the third century inscriptions of actors' guilds record a regular complement of three actors for tragedy and comedy.[14] However, there are three internal features of the extant comedies of Menander which point to an overall restriction

232–7; W. Stockert, *Aulularia* (Stuttgart, 1983) 13–16 summarizes recent views of the subject which overwhelmingly favour a Menandrean original.

[5] Identification with *Dis Exapaton* accepted since F. Ritschl, *Parergon Plautinorum Terentianorumque*, i (Leipzig, 1845), 404–12.

[6] See D. K. Lange, *CJ* 70. 3 (1975), 30–2.

[7] Cf. didascalia 'GRAECA ADELPHOE MENANDRU'.

[8] Cf. prologue 9 'Menander fecit Andriam et Perinthiam',

[9] Cf. didascalia 'GRAECA EST MENANDRU'.

[10] Cf. prologue 19–20 'quam nunc acturi sumus | Menandri Eunuchum'.

[11] Cf. didascalia 'GRAECA MENANDRU'.

[12] K. Gaiser, *Poetica*, 1 (1967), 436–7, argues that this may be the case with Plautus' *Miles Gloriosus*.

[13] Sandbach (1975) 197 distinguishes between a restriction on more than three actors speaking in any scene and more than three speaking actors featuring in a play: the following discussion concentrates on the latter rule, since it would, as Sandbach remarks, imply and explain the former (which would otherwise be nothing more than an aesthetic principle).

[14] For the ancient evidence and a discussion see A. W. Pickard-Cambridge, *The Dramatic Festivals of Athens*[2] (Oxford, 1968), 135ff.; N. C. Hourmouziades, *GRBS* 14 (1973), 185–8.

to three speaking actors. First, no scene yet discovered requires more than three speakers, and the amount of text extant suggests that this is not merely coincidental.[15] Secondly, Menander not infrequently brings on to the stage a character who does not speak throughout his scene yet whose actual silence is concealed in a variety of ingenious ways: for example an entrance apparently in mid-conversation with a speaking character is used repeatedly to convey the impression that the mute partner has spoken just prior to entry,[16] or a speaker may interpret a mute's gesture[17] or mime[18] in the place of speech. If no such restriction on the number of speakers existed, it would have been more simple and straightforward to supply such minor characters with small speaking parts. Thirdly, in a number of scenes exits of speakers that appear to be unexpectedly early invariably take place shortly before the arrival of another speaking character:[19] the need to deploy only three actors to play all the speaking roles would provide an explanation for this phenomenon, which allows time for changes of costume and position for re-entry in another role.[20]

A necessary consequence of recognizing a three-actor rule is the acceptance of part-splitting, whereby a character is played by more than one speaking actor in the course of the play:[21] to make this practice acceptable to the audience, the actors involved would require skill in conveying by voice and movement a uniform impression of the character (although this would be aided to a large degree by a distinctive mask and costume).

A(2) *Mutes*

Mutes may perform two types of role in Menander: specific individual characters, or attendants and stage-hands.[23] The former category

[15] Cf. GS 17.

[16] See below, B(6)(*d*).

[17] Cf. GS on *Epitr.* 1120.

[18] Cf. GS on *Mis.* 208.

[19] GS, pp. 17–18, collect some examples; see also F. H. Sandbach, *The Comic Theatre of Greece and Rome* (London, 1977), 79–80.

[20] Cf. Webster (1974) 82–3. The controversial passage at *Sik.* 271–2 leaves on one interpretation no time for such a change, and so would require four speaking actors: however, other solutions with less radical implications are equally possible (see note ad loc. in the second part).

[21] Cf. Hourmouziades (op. cit. n. 14) 179–81.

[22] Cf. GS 18; Sandbach (op. cit. n. 19) 80.

[23] On mutes in earlier Greek drama see D. P. Stanley-Porter, *BICS* 20 (1973), 68–93; Taplin (1977) 78–80. Bain (1981) 44–7 has some interesting remarks on slaves in comedy.

includes both non-speaking characters, who are usually left unnamed (for example, the cook's slave at *Aspis* 222 and Syriskos' wife in *Epitr.* ii), and split parts where a character is, owing to the restraints of the three-actor rule, shared between speaking and non-speaking actors. In all such cases the care taken in handling their movements on and off the stage is essentially the same as that applied to speakers. When mutes in the latter category appear not as individual characters but as attendants—for example, baggage-carriers and captives (*Aspis* 1–2), porters (*Sam.* 96–7), or helpers for a proposed siege (*Perik.* 477)—their obvious degree of involvement in the dramatic action is such that their presence and movements are normally in no doubt. However, in a number of passages the usual clear textual indications of when and from where an entrance takes place, and in what way and for how long the entrant is occupied, are almost entirely absent. These passages are found when slaves are given instructions to fetch and carry which are issued in an impersonal form using τιϲ and a third-person imperative, a device inherited from earlier drama:[24] they may be ordered to bring something, often torches or garlands at the end of a play,[25] to remove people or items,[26] or to summon others.[27] Sometimes the issuing of such an order appears as the first indication in the text that anyone other than the speakers should be supposed to be on-stage, presumably standing silently in the background:[28] alternatively such orders may be imagined to be directed towards one of the houses, with the slave at once emerging from indoors to perform in silence and unremarked whatever is required.[29]

The almost total disregard for clarity in their whereabouts and movements, unique in Menander's presentation of exits and entrances, reflects the low dramatic importance of such 'fetch-and-carry' stage-hands: only once, at *Sam.* 732, does one receive an

[24] Cf. Eur. *IA* 617, 1462; *Hel.* 1431; *Bacch.* 346; *El.* 500, and see Stanley-Porter, *BICS* 20 (1973), 85 n. 41; Ar. *Ach.* 805; *Nub.* 1490; *Thesm.* 238, 265; *Ran.* 871; *Av.* 1579, 1693; *Vesp.* 529; *Plut.* 1194.

[25] *Dysk.* 963–4; *Sam.* 731; *Sik.* 418 (with Handley's supplement): cf. *CGF* 249. 13 δεῦ]ρό τιϲ ϲτε[φ]άνουϲ ταχὺ. At *Sam.* 321 a strap is ordered, but not brought; see note ad loc. in the second part of this book.

[26] *Aspis* 387; *Kith.* 51–2.

[27] *Perik.* 751, 1009.

[28] Cf. GS on *Perik.* 751.

[29] Contrast the practice of the Roman comedians who in the absence of a three-actor rule were not averse to giving small speaking parts to minor characters who in the Greek originals would almost certainly have been played by mutes; cf. Sandbach (1975) 199–200; Bain (1981) 46 n. 1.

entrance announcement. Their status and role may have been made clear to the audience by certain visual clues: G. M. Sifakis[30] has argued on the basis of mosaic representations of certain plays that in Menander's time mute slaves were played by boys without masks.

A(3) *Wing Entrances*

Where plays are set in Athens, harbour and city are assumed to lie to the spectators' right, the country to their left: for a discussion of the evidence see below on *Sam.* 96.

B. ENTRANCES AND ENTRANCE MOTIVATIONS

B(1) *Visual Announcements*

In both frequency and form visual announcements in Menander invite direct comparison with the practice of earlier drama. Indeed, a recent examination of the technique of fifth-century tragedy reaches conclusions equally valid for the fourth-century comedian: 'most announcements contain at least two of the following standard elements: announcing particles (καὶ μήν, ἀλλὰ γάρ), deictic pronoun, name, reference to the entering character's movement, reference to the announcer's perception of the arrival'.[31] The basic similarities are easily illustrated: deictic pronouns are commonly used to draw attention to an approaching character[32] and while καὶ μήν does not feature in announcements in extant Menander, ἀλλὰ γάρ is found at least three times,[33] as is καὶ γάρ.[34]

With the exception of the two announcements at *Perin.* 7 and 9, where the slave's attention is firmly fixed on his master's door in terrified expectation of Laches' return,[35] visual announcements in the extant Menander all concern entrances from the sides. The interval between the moment at which an approaching character is sighted and

[30] 'Boy Actors in New Comedy', in G. W. Bowersock *et al.* (edd.), *Arktouros: Hellenic Studies Presented to B. M. W. Knox* (New York, 1979), 199–208.

[31] R. Hamilton, *HSPh* 82 (1978), 63 n. 1.

[32] *Aspis* 430; *DE* 30 (?); *Dysk.* 47, 143, 607; *Epitr.* 576; *Sam.* 280, 639; *Sik.* 29 (?); cf. *PGhôran* ii. 77.

[33] *Dysk.* 607; *Sam.* 280, 639. The expression is discussed in more detail in the note on *DE* 30, which is another possible example.

[34] *Aspis* 246; *Dysk.* 47, 230. On the meaning of καὶ γάρ see J. Diggle, *Euripides'* Phaethon (Cambridge, 1970), 95 n. 1: '*καὶ γάρ* is used when a character remarks that the arrival of others signals that it is time for his own departure.'

[35] On the visual announcement of the stage-hand at *Sam.* 732 see A(2).

his reaching a position towards the centre of the stage at which contact with those present would be possible is variously filled:[36] there may be straightforward identification on a first appearance,[37] description of manner or mood,[38] or some comment on the timeliness of the entrance.[39] In cases of particularly detailed and so lengthy announcements where a specific effect is created such as tension,[40] or where the provision of background information allows a minimum of explanation when contact is made and consequently the swift communication of important news,[41] there appears to have been a convention inherited from fifth-century drama that the announcer could observe a character approaching long before he became visible to the audience.[42]

On the special class of first choral announcements see note on *Aspis* 249 in the second part of this book.

B(2) *Announcements Prompted by Door Noise*

The use of door noise to alert characters on stage to an imminent arrival is a device found first in the plays of Euripides: the naturalistic effect was adopted by Old Comedy and was by the time of Menander, as its frequent occurrence testifies, an accepted and familiar dramatic technique.[43] Like the visual announcement, its purpose is primarily to introduce an adjustment of the situation on stage in view of an imminent entrance, with the additional element that the identity of the entrant is unknown at the time of announcement.

In its simplest form this adjustment consists of focusing the audience's attention onto the new arrival and away from the characters on stage, bringing monologue or dialogue to a halt:[44] a more arresting

[36] Cf. Mastronade (1979) 20; Taplin (1977) 72.

[37] *Geo.* 32; *Dysk.* 47, 773; *Sik.* 29 (?).

[38] *Dysk.* 47, 147, 255; *Epitr.* 576; *Sam.* 59; *Sik.* 124.

[39] εἰϲ καλόν: *Dysk.* 773; *Sam.* 280. εἰϲ δέοντα . . . καιρόν: *Sam.* 639–40. Some similar expressions in earlier Greek drama are collected by W. Schmid, *Geschichte der Griechischen Literatur*, i. 2 (Munich, 1934), 75 n. 9; examples in Plautus and Terence are listed by Duckworth (1952) 115.

[40] The first appearance of Knemon (*Dysk.* 143–52); the return of Smikrines (*Epitr.* 576–82).

[41] *Sik.* 120–4.

[42] Cf. N. Hourmouziades, *Production and Imagination in Euripides* (Athens, 1965), 145; Taplin (1977) 72–3.

[43] For an account of the device and its development see Fraenkel (1912) 60–3.

[44] *Dysk.* 204; *Epitr.* 906; *Mis.* 282, 442; *Perik.* 316; *Sam.* 300, 532, 555, 567, 669; *CGF* 264.

effect results when the announcement actually interrupts a speech.[45] More complex techniques are also found where door noise provides a warning for a character on stage to perform, or cease, some action: it may act as a cue for withdrawal to observe the new arrival unseen,[46] prompt an actual exit,[47] or delay a movement to leave the stage.[48]

In describing door noise two verbs are used in virtually stereotyped phrases: ψοφεῖν[49] and πλήccειν.[50] Their precise meanings are explained most convincingly by Bader[51] who takes the former to refer to the sound of the door creaking on its pivots, and the latter to the noise of the door banging against its frame, being momentarily pushed forwards as the handle is seized from inside prior to its being flung open. The apparent distinction governing the choice of verb is that phrases featuring πλήccειν reflect some excitement on the part of the new entrant, whose haste produces the banging noise;[52] but this is not inflexible, as Bader[53] notes that phrases featuring ψοφεῖν may also be used of excited entrances (e.g. *Dysk.* 586; *Sam.* 567).

B(3) *Entry Talking Back*

Scenes in which a character enters the stage while delivering a few words back into the house to an unseen addressee are frequent in the extant Menander. The technique, which was of comparatively recent origin,[54] offered dramatic possibilities which New Comedy exploited to the full. Since the new entrant emerges still in contact with the imagined scene indoors, it was possible to convey to the audience a vivid impression of that scene—the grief of a household over some misfortune,[55] the bustle of preparations for a feast,[56] or the acrimony of an angry argument.[57] As a further consequence, the entrant's attention is initially directed back into the house and so away from the situation

[45] *Dysk.* 586, 689; cf. *CGF* 264.

[46] *Karch.* 4; *Mis.* 206; *Sam.* 336.

[47] *Epitr.* 874; *Perik.* 1003.

[48] *Dysk.* 188.

[49] Transitive: *Dysk.* 204, 586, 689; *Epitr.* 875; *Karch.* 4; *Mis.* 206, 282, 442; *Perik.* 316; *Sam.* 669. Intransitive: *Sam.* 567; cf. *Perik.* 1004.

[50] *Dysk.* 188; *Epitr.* 906; *Sam.* 300, 366, 555.

[51] B. Bader, *Antichthon*, 5 (1971), 41, 48. See also H. Petersmann, *WS* 5 (1971), 91–109.

[52] cf. GS on *Sam.* 300–1.

[53] Op. cit. 48.

[54] The only example in fifth-century drama is found at Ar. *Ach.* 1003–4; cf. Legrand (1910) 449; Harms (1914) 31 n. 1.

[55] *Aspis* 164, 223: *Sam.* 440.

[56] *Dysk.* 546; *Sam.* 198, 301.

[57] *Dysk.* 487; *Sam.* 713.

on stage: this fact is used at *Epitr.* 430 to introduce a scene of mutual unawareness as Habrotonon, concerned to ward off the unwanted attentions of party guests, fails at first to see Onesimos; while at *Perik.* 181 Doris' entrance talking back to Glykera explains her failure to see Sosias watching her.

As an alternative to the common entrance monologue, the device provides a more vivid means for the explicit statement of entrance motivation in the form of a direct address to whoever has either prompted, or is otherwise closely involved in, the movement from the house.[58] Not infrequently, however, where a character is required on-stage for a particular scene to be presented to the audience, and yet no naturalistic reason exists for him at that moment to leave his house, the address back through the door can conceal the absence of any actual motivation, as the audience's attention is engaged by the content of his remarks and, on occasions, the emotion with which they are delivered.[59]

B(4) *Entry in Search of Another*

A number of important scenes which rely on purely coincidental but timely meetings on stage are brought about when one character enters with the express purpose of finding another. The majority of examples follow the same basic pattern; the new entrant at once makes his motivation explicit in a brief entrance monologue, only to find his quarry already present.[60] In this group there is a discernible tendency towards a verbal stereotype, as all the examples except *Mis.* 216 feature entrance monologues based on ποῦ ἐϲτί ('where is he?'; cf. Blundell (1980) 12[61]). The remaining cases diverge from the above pattern in

[58] *Aspis* 299; *Dysk.* 456, 487, 874, 879; *Epitr.* 430, 853 (?); *Perik.* 181, 366; *Sam.* 421; *Sik.* 37. (At Ter. *An.* 490–1 Simo measures the nurse's entrance talking back by the standards of real life and concludes that it is a crude attempt to deceive him into believing in the recent birth. This comic treatment of the conventional entrance may derive from the Greek original; cf. Fraenkel (1922) 144; Gomme (1937) 260 n. 1; S. M. Goldberg, *C&M* 33 (1982) 138.)

[59] *Aspis* 164; *Dysk.* 546; *Mis.* 276; *Sam.* 440, 713. In the Latin versions cf. Plaut. *Bacch.* 179, where Pistoclerus' timely but unexplained appearance, leaving his disapproving tutor Lydus alone in the brothel, leads to a meeting with the slave Chrysalus; *Stich.* 523, where Epignomus conveniently but without explanation enters to find Pamphilippus and Antipho on stage; Ter. *An.* 842, where Davos, required on-stage for a scene with Chremes and Simo, fails to explain why he leaves the happy reunion inside the house.

[60] *DE* 102; *Dysk.* 588; *Epitr.* 442; *Mis.* 216; *Sam.* 690.

[61] Compare in Terence the frequent use in such circumstances of the phrases 'ubi est' or 'ubi quaeram'; *Ad.* 265, 359, 924; *An.* 338, 607, 965; *Eun.* 643, 1006, 1050. See also Pl. *Men.* 357.

various ways: the entrance monologues at *Kith.* 53 and 66 are both lengthy, and in neither case is the speaker's quarry already present on-stage when he arrives, while at *Sam.* 357 the cook is unsuccessful in locating Parmenon. Note also *Epitr.* 142 where a resumption of contact rather than a search takes place.

B(5) *Entry in Response to Summons*

(*a*) *Door-knocking*. A brief survey of earlier drama shows that the act of summoning a character from his house by knocking at his door had by Menander's time acquired a number of comic associations. Few examples of knocking are to be found in fifth-century tragedy,[62] where a purely verbal summons at the door is much more frequent:[63] probably this was due to the popularity of knocking, with its scope for farce and slapstick, in Old Comedy,[64] as a result of which it was considered unsuitable for serious drama.[65]

In extant Menander, the humorous element of door-knocking is exploited in the ham-fisted approaches made to Knemon at *Dysk.* 458 and 498 (note also 911 ff.), and also at *Epitr.* 1075 where Smikrines' indignant knocking leads into his comic discomfiture.[66] However, a wish to avoid the comic associations of the device may provide a partial explanation at least for the two cases of door-knocking which are for various reasons and at various stages broken off before completion, *Aspis* 162 and *Mis.* 206: here Menander may have been reluctant to introduce scenes of serious content by action which was widely associated with humour, even though his efforts to avoid the knocking sequence result in somewhat implausible action in each case. Only once in the extant comedies is knocking successfully carried out in a serious scene (*Aspis* 499) where the door is, apparently, immediately answered at the first knock.[67]

(*b*) *Summoning by a Shout*. This straightforward technique needs little comment: since a verbal summons by its very nature implies an

[62] Taplin (1977) 340–1 discusses possible cases.

[63] Mooney (1914) 19–20 gives examples.

[64] Cf. Petersmann (op. cit. n. 51) 91 n. 3.

[65] Taplin (1977) 341.

[66] Here and at *Aspis* 499 the use of παίειν rather than the usual κόπτειν reflects the urgency of the knocker, an effect enhanced in both cases by the use of the verbal adjectives; cf. GS on *Aspis* 499.

[67] Two further associated passages are uninformative: at *Dysk.* 267 Sostratos is distracted as soon as he announces his intention to knock; at *Perik.* 184 the text is too fragmentary to be of any value.

exercise of authority by the speaker, in the majority of cases the relationship involved is either that of master and slave[68] or of social equals[69] one of whom temporarily assumes control. Only once (*Dysk.* 635) is a social superior, Gorgias, summoned by an inferior, Simiche: there the transgression of the normal social limits on the device serves to underline the old woman's extreme distress at a moment of crisis.

B(6) *Entry in Mid-conversation*

Entrances of two characters engaged in a conversation apparently begun off-stage are common in Menander, although they feature far less often in fifth-century drama.[70] The impression that the audience is hearing only a section from a continuous dialogue may be conveyed in a variety of different ways:

(*a*) *Syntax*. Reference is made to earlier conversation by the use of connective particles.[71]

(*b*) *The apistetic question*.[72] Questions whose purpose 'is to express disbelief, surprise, shock or dismay' may introduce a brief recapitulation of the conversation so far.[73]

(*c*) *Clear reference to the partner's earlier words*. This may take the form of a direct quotation[74] or of a less explicit remark.[75]

(*d*) *Content and context*. On occasions none of the above pointers is given, but there is no doubt that a conversation (often an argument) is in progress.[76]

Besides its straightforward function as the regular means by which two characters may be brought on to the stage together, entry in mid-conversation can be used to circumvent some restrictions of dramatic convention. First, the fact that no indoor scenes could be shown posed

[68] *Sam.* 189 (Demeas to Parmenon); *Sik.* 385 (Stratophanes to Donax). Note also *Sam.* 730 (Demeas to his social inferior Chrysis), and those passages featuring mute slaves discussed at A(2).

[69] *Dysk.* 637, 889.

[70] Cf. Taplin (1977) 363–4, *GRBS* 12 (1971), 40; F. Leo, *NGG* 10 (1905), 42–3.

[71] εἶἑν: *Aspis* 250; ἀλλά: *Geo.* 22; *Epitr.* 714; (*Eunouchos* fr. 161 K.-T. may be a further example, although in Terence's version it is uncertain whether the corresponding opening speech of Phaedria (46–7) is delivered to Parmeno or is self-address (see B. Bader, *RhM* 116 (1973), 54–9); if the latter, then in the original ἀλλά may have begun a monologue, as at Ar. *Lys.* 1); δέ: *Dysk.* 233; οὐκοῦν: *Sam.* 96, 369.

[72] The terminology and definition are those of Mastronarde (1979) 12.

[73] *Dysk.* 50, 233; *Mis.* 259; *Sam.* 61.

[74] *Perik.* 1006.

[75] *Epitr.* 1063; *Perik.* 269; *Sam.* 285.

[76] *Dysk.* 611, 784; *Epitr.* 218; *Mis.* 270; *Heros* 1; *Sik.* 150, 272, 312.

the problem of how to move conversations which would naturally take place within the house out to the stage. By bringing characters on in the middle of an argument, it was possible to engage the audience's attention by the arresting manner of the entrance and so conceal the complete lack of any genuine motivation for the move from the house.[77] Secondly, the suggestion by one of the dialogue partners that his companion had spoken just prior to appearance could be used to conceal the fact that the latter was, under the constraints of the three-actor rule, played in the scene by a mute.[78] However, an obvious drawback of the device is the danger of implausibility from the requirement for the conversation to have reached that part which is of interest to the audience at the exact moment when the two characters enter the stage:[79] in the majority of cases this is handled without awkwardness, but one exception comes at *Dysk.* 233 (see GS ad loc.).

B(7) *Implicit Announcement*[80]

Where there is no explicit announcement of an entrance, mention may be made of the character who is about to appear by those on stage in conversation or monologue, thus preparing the way for his arrival and often providing essential background information or highlighting some other fact necessary for full appreciation of the following scene. Taplin (1977) 137–8 discusses this technique in Greek drama and distinguishes two categories, those where a person is mentioned with no suggestion of his imminent arrival, and those where an arrival is actually expected. A clear example of the first category comes at *Aspis* 399 where Smirkines has just delivered a speech on his opinion of Daos and his confidence that he is fully aware of his tricks: at this very moment the slave rushes on to set his scheme in motion. Later at *Aspis* 430 the entry of Chaireas and the false doctor comes just at the point when Smikrines has asked about medical attention for the stricken Chairestratos, an arrival whose convenience strengthens the impression that Daos will succeed with his plan.[81] The clearest example from

[77] *Dysk.* 784; *Epitr.* 714; *Perik.* 708 (?).

[78] *Epitr.* 1062; *Mis.* 206, 259; *Perik.* 1006: see A(1).

[79] Cf. Legrand (1910) 459ff. For examples in tragedy see Flickinger (1936) 259–60.

[80] In such cases the term 'talk-of-the-devil announcements' is now gaining currency (see Taplin (1977) 138; M. R. Halleran, *MSPh* 86 (1982), 282), but seems less accurate since only at Ter. *Ad.* 537 does a character actually make a comment of that type.

[81] Cf. also *Aspis* 234 (the entrance of the waiter as the cook has just abused him); *DE* 102 (the arrival of Moschos just as Sostratos' thoughts have turned to his friend's role in the supposed treachery).

the second category, an expected arrival which then takes place, comes at *Dysk.* 78 where Pyrrhias bursts on to the scene just as Sostratos and Chaireas are wondering at his lateness in returning; cf. *Kith.* 66 where Moschion enters just as his father has gone indoors to search for him.

B(8) *Wholly Unannounced Entrances*

Entrances may be completely unannounced for a variety of reasons. Self-evidently, appearances on an empty stage cannot be announced: but where the stage is already occupied, there may be a specific reason for leaving the arrival unremarked. The device is not uncommon: for instance, characters on stage may be absorbed in their own thoughts[82] or in conversation,[83] and an unnoticed entrance simply highlights the depths of their absorption. Occasionally, however, the abrupt effect of such a surprise appearance is designed specifically to grip the audience's attention: at *Perik.* 774, for example, Moschion arrives on-stage as his yet-unknown father and sister examine the recognition tokens, and his appearance adds an extra dimension to this crucial scene. At *Sam.* 440 Demeas bursts angrily from his house as Nikeratos relates to a bewildered Moschion the series of extraordinary events since he was last at home, a sudden and dramatic appearance which ushers in a scene of confused confrontation among the three main characters.[84]

C. EXITS AND EXIT MOTIVATIONS

C(1) *The Clear Exit-line*

The most frequent method of introducing a departure from the stage involves an explicit statement of intent which leaves the motivation and timing of the movement in no doubt: the exit may follow directly on delivery of the line or may be delayed briefly to allow either the speaker to finish his speech or for others on stage to react to the imminent departure. The device presents few problems and needs no detailed comment.[85]

[82] *Aspis* 216; *Epitr.* 430; *Mis.* A15; *Perik.* 181, 354; *Sam.* 357, 399, 428.

[83] *Perik.* 774; *Sam.* 440; *Sik.* 361.

[84] See further *Dysk.* 430, where the family group unexpectedly floods on to the stage before the enraged and misanthropic Knemon; *Dysk.* 574 (the dramatic appearance of Simiche); *Sik.* 169 (the arresting entrance of the messenger to delay 'Smikrines' ' exit).

[85] Lines signalling imminent departure indoors commonly use εἴϲω with a verb of motion. Εἴϲω with εἶμι: *Epitr.* 161; *Kith.* 63; *Mis.* 264, 451; *Perik.* 396, 1005; *Sam.* 196;

C(2) *Exit Instructions*

A large number of exits are introduced by an order to depart, and since this implies an exercise of authority by the issuer over the recipient, the majority of exits under orders are made by slaves or junior family-members.[86] In the comparatively few examples where this is not the case, the reason is usually obvious. For example, in certain situations one social equal may assume control over another when the actions being performed clearly fall within his province: at *Dysk.* 419 as the equipment for the feast is carried to the cave the cook, who is on any account a low-life character,[87] is naturally in charge of Getas the slave; and at *Sam.* 295 the slave Parmenon, having just led the hired cook to his master's house, instructs him to take his equipment inside.[88] Urgency or eagerness may also prompt instructions from a social equal[89] or, indeed, inferior.[90] However, in some cases the instruction constitutes polite encouragement or suggestion rather than actual or intended order (for example, the request of Getas the respected family slave (cf. 181–2) to the young master Sostratos at *Dysk.* 556, and Sostratos' instruction to his father (*Dysk.* 780) to enter and have lunch[91]).

Phasma 91. Εἴσω with other verbs: *Aspis* 91–2, 96; *Dysk.* 758; *Mis.* 173–5. Lines without εἴσω: *Geo.* 84; *Dysk.* 455, 478, 859, 883–4; *Epitr.* 170–1, 580, 857; *Perik.* 184, 298; *Sam.* 195, 694. Lines signalling departure to the side use a variety of verbs: *Aspis* 211–13, 377; *Geo.* 20; *DE* 89; *Dysk.* 144, 215–17, 378; *Epitr.* 463; *Perik.* 264; *Sam.* 94–5, 162 (?), 539; *Sik.* 271 (?).

86 Masters to slaves: *DE* 14; *Dysk.* 439, 589, 618–19; *Perik.* 295, 310, 755, 982; *Perin.* 1; *Sam.* 104, 202, 297, 658, 678; *Sik.* 145, 385. Senior to junior family-members: *Geo.* 39–40 (Daos is clearly a more senior slave in the household); *Dysk.* 698; *Epitr.* 405; *Sam.* 569–70; *Sik.* 311 (?). Others: *Dysk.* 866 (Sostratos to Gorgias' mother and sister); *Mis.* 274 (Kleinias to the hired cook); *Perik.* 481 (Pataikos to the parasite Sosias); *Sam.* 418 (Nikeratos to the hetaera Chrysis).

87 On the social status of cooks see GS, p. 131.

88 Cf. *Dysk.* 852, where Sostratos assumes the dominant role over Gorgias in issuing invitations to the wedding feast.

89 *Dysk.* 906 (Getas urging Sikon to enter and fetch Knemon: Handley (1965) ad loc. defines this as a 'conventional courtesy'); *Perik.* 525, where Polemon is eager for his friend to see Glykera's finery: *Sam.* 517 (Demeas is keen for Nikeratos to expel Chrysis); *Sik.* 364 (Dromon urges Theron to help the stricken Kichesias).

90 *DE* 59–60, where indignation prompts Sostratos to order his father to follow him indoors; *Epitr.* 876 (the capable Habrotonon instructs the bewildered Pamphile to lead the way indoors); *Perik.* 348–9, 351 (the scheming slave Daos is keen for Moschion to leave to give himself time to devise some further plan); *Sik.* 382 (the faint and still dazed Kichesias is swept off to be reunited with his daughter by the eager slave Dromon).

91 Cf. also *Dysk.* 781 (Gorgias urging Sostratos to approach his father), 871 (Sostratos' suggestion to Gorgias); *Epitr.* 168 (Habrotonon's suggestion to Charisios); *Kith.* 49–50

Exit instructions are generally obeyed in silence, but there are cases where the recipient gives an acknowledgement of the order before leaving. Such acknowledgement may serve one of two purposes: either to reassure an indignant or anxious instructor that the required action is in fact being performed,[92] or to reflect the eagerness of the speaker to carry out his mission.[93]

C(3) *Lines Spoken to a Departing Character*

When dialogue finishes and one character moves away to leave the stage, the other who remains may call after him for one of two possible reasons: either a confrontation has just ended, and the departing character goes off in defeat as the victor stays to vaunt over his repulsed opponent by insulting him; or the addressee may be on a mission about which the speaker is keen to encourage him or speed him on his way. In each case the remarks go unanswered.[94]

Fifth-century drama makes considerable use of the device, with tragedy favouring the insult[95] and Aristophanes an address of encouragement.[96] The preference displayed by Old Comedy was apparently shared by Menander, in whose extant plays only three examples of the device out of a total of fourteen involve insult: *Epitr.* 376 (Syriskos' contemptuous dismissal of the grumbling Daos), *Perik.* 526 (Moschion's empty bravado against Polemon and Pataikos from a safe distance), and *Sik.* 167 ('Smikrines' ' scornful boast to his departing dialogue partner). The remaining eleven cases all feature various degrees of encouragement or good wishes, and are mostly straightforward.[97] One example deserves some further comment: at *Dysk.* 426 the cook instructs Getas to follow him into the cave and the slave, remaining behind, assures him of his confidence in him, waiting until his addressee has disappeared inside to turn his praise into an insult.[98]

(B's suggestion to A); *Sam.* 612–13, 723 (the polite and carefully phrased requests by Demeas to Nikeratos).

[92] *DE* 59; *Perik.* 295, 310, 481, 525; *Sam.* 389, 663, 680; cf. *PGhôran* ii. 179.

[93] *Dysk.* 699, 780; *Perik.* 351; *Sam.* 612.

[94] Cf. the observation of Mastronarde (1979) 30 (on the device in tragedy, but equally applicable to New Comedy): 'turning from dialogue contact to depart conventionally renders aural contact void or imperfect, regardless of the actual physical proximity of the departing character'.

[95] Taplin (1977) 221–2 gives examples and discussion.

[96] Taplin (1977) 22.

[97] *Aspis* 93–4, 379; *Dysk.* 213, 860, 884–5; *Epitr.* 370, 414; *Mis.* 238; *Perik.* 299; *Sam.* 614a.

[98] For the manner of delivery compare in the Latin versions the following: Plaut.

C(4) *Delayed Exits*

A delayed exit takes place when an announced or actual exit movement is halted either by outside intervention or by second thoughts on the part of the character himself. Most of the examples in Menander can be divided into two groups:[99] delays which contribute to characterization and those which introduce important scenes. Examples in the former group follow a standard pattern: one speaker instructs another to follow him off the stage, but his companion fails to comply and raises some momentary objection whose purpose is, apparently, to cast light on his own character.[100] The technique used in exits of the latter group has its origins in fifth-century tragedy:[101] the visually impressive scene which results when a movement to depart is interrupted by some unexpected external intervention is used to grip the audience's attention and to introduce an important episode. One clear example comes at *Epitr.* 858–9 where Habrotonon's call to Pamphile, who is about to enter the house, causes a delayed exit which leads on to the recognition of the girl as the previously violated mother of the baby; this use of the technique is not uncommon in the extant plays.[102]

C(5) *Relegation or Omission of Exit-line*

In a number of exits the statement of intent to leave which normally makes the movement explicit in the text is either relegated to a

Bacch. 1066–7: NI. cura hoc. iam ego huc revenero. | CH. curatum est—esse te senem miserrumum; *Cist.* 595–6: LA. perfectum ego hoc dabo negotium. | PH. deos teque spero.—LA. eosdem ego—uti abeas domum. Ter. *Ad.* 587 may be a further example: i sane: ego te exercebo hodie, ut dignus es, silicernium. However, the punctuation is uncertain, and it may be that none of the line is intended for Demea's ears; see R. Kauer, *WS* 22 (1900), 108.

[99] An exception is *Sik.* 365 where the delay to Theron's exit merely contributes to the farcical bustle of the scene.

[100] *DE* 15 (Lydos wants to stay and help chastise Moschos), 59 (Sostratos' father is incredulous at the story he has just been told); *Dysk.* 871 (Gorgias experiences embarrassment at meeting strange women socially); *Sik.* 145 (Theron tries to learn more about the letter Stratophanes has received). Note also *DE* 23, where Sostratos, alone on stage and overcome by doubts, delays his own movement to knock on his beloved's door.

[101] Cf. Taplin (1977), 162–3.

[102] *Aspis* 455–6; *Dysk.* 181, 574; *Epitr.* 364; *Sam.* 295; *Sik.* 169. A similar effect is achieved at *Dysk.* 269 where Sostratos' move to knock at Knemon's door is interrupted by the intervention of Gorgias.

secondary position or completely omitted. As a result the words spoken just before the speaker leaves the stage are given a certain prominence which lends them emphasis and can be used to considerable dramatic effect; cf. the remarks of Gilula (1979) 521 on this technique. This is a common device in Menander, and some of the more notable examples of it are examined in section (*a*) below: cases where the exit is remarked on or acknowledged by a character who remains on-stage are discussed in section (*b*).

(*a*) *Unacknowledged Exits.* Where an explicit exit line occurs but is relegated to a position of secondary importance, the actual intent to leave is plain enough and only the precise timing may cause momentary difficulty for the reader. For example, at *Dysk.* 479b–80 Getas' clear exit-line (478–9a) is relegated in favour of his insulting description of Knemon which is delivered with emphasis as his parting words. The prominent position is also exploited at *Epitr.* 555–6 where Habrotonon, whose departure as soon as Onesimos has handed her the ring has been expected since 514–15, speaks a heartfelt prayer to Persuasion as she leaves.[103]

The wholesale omission of a statement of intent to leave can be used to even greater dramatic effect and is commonly found in scenes of high emotion where an explicit exit-line would sound unrealistic or stilted. For example, at *Sam.* 398a Demeas finishes his furious tirade against Chrysis with the order ἔϲταθι ('stay there') at which he rushes back indoors, leaving her on stage: in his anger it is not surprising that he fails to give a clear exit-line.[104] Alternatively, characters may leave stressing their feelings of exasperation or hopelessness in their parting words, as does Chairestratos at *Aspis* 282–3: this emotional effect is exploited by Daos at *Aspis* 432 when, as part of the fiction that Chairestratos is seriously ill, he follows the 'doctor' inside with a quotation from Euripides.[105] The device may also be found at act or scene endings, where the last character to leave the stage delivers a brief monologue rounding off the section.[106]

[103] Cf. *Dysk.* 202–3, 572–3.

[104] Further examples of angry exits which use this technique are *Dysk.* 481–6 (Knemon's lengthy condemnation of his fellow men), and *Dysk.* 600–1 (his parting curse on Getas).

[105] Note the emotional use of ὢ in the examples at *Dysk.* 178, 514; *Mis.* 258; *Perik.* 360.

[106] e.g. *Dysk.* 391–2, 664–5; *Epitr.* 416–18; *Sam.* 614–15.

(*b*) *Acknowledged Exits.* An exit may be remarked upon by a character who remains for two possible reasons. First, if the departure is made in silence, this remark or acknowledgement constitutes the first explicit indication in the text that an exit has taken place.[107] Secondly, when the general intention to leave is plain enough but the parting words spoken are used not to form a clear exit-line but to shed light on speaker's thoughts or emotions,[108] the exit acknowledgement not only clarifies for the reader the exact moment of departure, but may also be used in performance to comment on the manner of the exit, or the speaker's reaction to it, or both.[109]

[107] *Perik.* 984 (Doris' silent obedience of Polemon). Another example may come at *Perik.* 384, but see note ad loc.

[108] *DE* 14–18 (Lydos' anxiety); *Dysk.* 600–2 (Knemon's rage); *Sam.* 359–61 (Demeas' fury), 547, 563 (Nikeratos' grim single-mindedness).

[109] See notes on *DE* 17; *Dysk.* 134, 601; *Sam.* 360–1, 563. Exit acknowledgement in Roman Comedy is used to create comparable effects; cf. Plaut. *Aul.* 244, 265, 460; *Bacch.* 905; *Cist.* 528, 650; *Stich.* 632; Ter. *Ad.* 782; *Hec.* 444, 510; *HT* 975. Note the predominance of the perfect tense of 'abeo' in these examples.

THE EXTANT PLAYS

1
Aspis

1. *Enter captives* (36–7) *from the harbour with pack animals loaded with booty* (140–1); DAOS *follows carrying a battered shield* (15–17), *accompanied by* SMIKRINES, *who remains in the background*

The opening scene is likely to have come as a complete contradiction to the audience's expectations of a New Comedy play. First, their interest is engaged by the arresting manner in which the stage is filled by a silent procession of captives before Daos emerges with the battered shield whose significance is soon to become clear;[1] secondly, the old slave's monologue contains not the ingredients of a lover's intrigue but the wholly serious report of a death. His speech is serious in tone and form. The first nine lines are in tragic rather than comic metre,[2] and Daos presents a contrast of former hopes and present realities which was a conventional feature of laments in Greek literature:[3] ὡς τότ' ἤλπις' ('as I hoped then', 3) νῦν δέ ('but now', 13). This predominantly serious atmosphere lasts until the delayed divine prologue explains the true state of affairs, and ensures the audience's interest in Daos' story:[4] at the same time the opening eighteen lines are put to good use in sketching in background details as the slave explains Kleostratos' mission abroad (8–10) and his own relationship to him, 'tutor' (14) to 'young master' (2).

The whereabouts of Smikrines has caused some difficulty. GS ad loc. remark that the first verbal contact (18–21) does not suggest that this is the point at which he meets Daos for the first time on his

[1] The order in which the captives and Daos enter the stage is unclear from the text as it survives and indeed GS suggest that Daos enters first: however, Arnott (1979) has Daos following the crowd, and Sandbach (in A. Blanchard, *Essai sur la composition des comédies de Ménandre* (Paris, 1983), 149 n. 59) now agrees: 'Did not the procession come first, arousing the audience's curiosity? Then the climax is the entry of Daos, carrying the shield, which must be another cause for curiosity: all attention is concentrated on Daos, whose words first give a hint, then a clear implication of what had happened.'

[2] Cf. Sandbach (1970) 133.

[3] M. Alexiou, *The Ritual Lament in Greek Tradition* (Cambridge, 1974), 165–6, 175; Blundell (1980) 71–3.

[4] Cf. Holzberg (1974) 28.

homecoming and, although he need only hear 13ff. to realize that Kleostratos is believed to be dead, it appears unlikely that Smikrines enters silently from his house during Daos' speech: if he were brought out by the noise of the arrival, he might be expected to make this clear (for a possible method cf. *Fab. Inc.* 20). If Smikrines and Daos enter together, the depth of the slave's grief would account for his disregard of Smikrines during his lament, and the audience would assume they have already met off-stage.

When Smikrines addresses him, Daos' style of expression descends from its elevated height and metre to a more everyday level:[5] the old man now performs a quasi-protatic role,[6] breaking up Daos' lengthy account of his master's 'death' with brief questions and remarks.

91–6. DAOS. Let us go inside to tell this wretched story to those who ought least to hear it.

Exit DAOS *to* CHAIRESTRATOS' *house, followed by the captives.*

SMIKRINES [*calling after him as he goes*]. Then I shall want to talk to you, Daos, about something at leisure. [*To himself*] But now I think I too will go indoors to consider in what way one could deal most gently with these people.

[*Exit* SMIKRINES *to his house*

Daos goes to tell the household of his master's supposed death (91–2). Smikrines addresses 93–4a to Daos, and these words go unacknowledged: either then the slave stays to hear them and turns to go at 94a in silence (cf. Bain (1977) 132–3) or, as indicated above, he may leave at the end of 92 with Smikrines calling after him. The remainder of the old man's words constitute soliloquy (94a–96) and Daos will in any case not hear them, whether off stage already or on the point of entering the house. (The marginal note in the papyrus ηϲυχη by 93 wrongly suggests an aside in Daos' presence; cf. Bain (1977) 132–3.)

Smikrines' reasons for leaving are clear from 94b–96: he wishes to consider how to approach Kleostratos' family ἡμερώτατα ('most gently'). As GS remark ad loc., the word used is 'emphatic by its position' and the audience might wonder how such an approach accords with the old man's portrayal so far, which has been consistently negative: his reaction to the 'death' was that it was merely ἀνελπίϲτοϲ ('unexpected') leaving Daos to express the horror of it

[5] Cf. Sandbach (1970) 133.

[6] Cf. S. Ireland, *Hermes*, 109 (1981), 180.

(18–19). In the lines immediately preceding his exit the slave has made his opinion of Smikrines clear—he is only interested in inheriting the booty (κληρονόμε 'heir to the estate', 85; emphatic οἰκεῖον 'your very own', 89). Smikrines' exit-line adds an element of mystery as his plans are as yet unknown, and the need for a 'gentle' approach only increases the suspense.

97. *Enter* TYCHE

The text provides no indication of the direction of Tyche's entrance, and the problem has been overlooked by editors and commentators. Unlike an initial divine prologue where the speaker, before any human characters have appeared, prefaces the action and so is divorced from it, Tyche delivers a delayed prologue which is flanked by the appearance of mortals, and it may be worth considering whether her speech was delivered not on the stage itself but on an upper level such as that used for divine epiphanies in fifth-century tragedy (and particularly by Euripides[7]). However, since there is no certain evidence to support this proposal (the other extant delayed divine prologues in *Perik.* and *Phasma* are too incomplete to provide any corroboration) it may be that Tyche simply entered at stage level from one of the sides.[8]

The goddess keeps her precise identity secret until the very end of her speech (148). Her prologue dispels for the audience the air of gloom created by the opening scenes.[9] She plunges directly into her account,[10] and dismisses the beliefs of the mortal characters (99). When Tyche departs, she leves the audience in possession of all the facts necessary to appreciate the irony of the scenes to come.

148. *Exit* TYCHE

[7] On this feature of Euripides see W. S. Barrett, *Hippolytos* (Oxford, 1964) on 1283. The *skene* roof is a more likely location for such appearances than the special platform or θεολογεῖον described by the late encyclopaedist Pollux, on the inadequacy of whose testimony see Taplin (1977) 432–3: on the suitability of the *skene* roof, ibid. 440–1. Some such upper level was certainly available in the late fourth-century theatre, as the frequent revivals of Euripides attest.

[8] Cf. the remarks of Barrett (op. cit. n. 7) concerning the practice of Euripides: 'when gods appear in the prologue, with no mortals present, there is not the same need for them to be at a height: whether or not they appeared at ground level we have no means of telling'.

[9] Cf. Holzberg (1974) 29–30.

[10] Note the abrupt ἀλλά (97) and for the effect see E. Fraenkel, *Beobachtungen zu Aristophanes* (Rome, 1962), 103.

149. *Enter* SMIKRINES *from his house*
Smikrines' reason for emerging—to call out Daos (cf. 93)—is not given until 162–3, but the delay in stating his motivation is unlikely to concern the audience since the effect of his entrance monologue is above all comic: he enters still concerned with the booty that has been brought back, and prides himself that he cannot be called φιλάργυρος ('money-mad', 149), the exact term used of him by Tyche (123). His self-assurance could only amuse the audience which has just heard his final defeat predicted.

162–7. SMIKRINES. But nevertheless I'll knock on the door and call Daos out. He's the only one who'll attend to me.

As he moves towards CHAIRESTRATOS' *door* DAOS *appears at it, addressing his words back into the house.*

DAOS. I've much sympathy for your acting in this way, but in the circumstances you must take what's happened as reasonably as you can.

SMIKRINES. I've come for you, Daos.

DAOS. For me?

Daos enters unannounced and without motivation: he is not looking for Smikrines in obedience to his earlier request (93–4), and is surprised that Smikrines is looking for him (166–7). Menander has avoided using the obvious means to motivate his entry, a response to knocking on the door, since although Smikrines announces his intention to knock, Daos appears before the action can be performed,[11] and the dramatic convenience of the slave's independent entrance at precisely the moment when Smikrines is about to call him out might seem to strain the audience's credulity. However, Menander's arrangement of the scene produces positive dramatic gains which forestall any such objections: the playwright may have felt a door-knocking scene, which appears by this time to have been associated with comedy and slapstick,[12] to be inappropriate to introduce the confrontation of the loyal and grieving Daos and the greedy Smikrines; as a result the necessary meeting had to be brought

[11] Jacques (1978) 48 n. 22 suggests that Smikrines does knock at the door; but this is unlikely, since in all other Menandrean scenes of door-knocking there is some explicit verbal indication of the action, e.g. the knocker cries παῖ(δες) (*Dysk.* 459, 498; *Epitr.* 1075; *Mis.* 206; *Perik.* 188); or the door is answered with τίς τὴν θύραν (*Aspis* 499: a restoration by Austin, cf. *CGF* 368. 5–6).

[12] See B(5)(*a*) in the first part of this book.

about by some other means. The fact that the slave's appearance is unmotivated is concealed by the manner of his entry, speaking back to the women in the house (there are no men at home (213)), and this engages the audience's interest: entrances talking back frequently conceal weak or non-existent entry motivation.[13] The dramatic advantage of the arrangement is that if Daos opened the door in response to knocking by Smikrines, the confrontation would begin at once: an independent entry talking back means that the slave's period of unawareness of Smikrines' presence can be put to good use in demonstrating Daos' genuine loyalty and distress at his master's death (164–6a). In this way the audience is reminded of the contrast of his character and that of Smikrines before their meeting begins and the old man reveals his plan to obtain the booty by marriage.

213. *Exit* SMIKRINES *to the market-place*
Smikrines announces his intention to depart at 211 and may have guessed that the male family-members are not at home from Daos' address back into the house at 164ff. (so GS ad loc.): when Daos confirms this with οὐδεῖϲ ('no one', 213), Smikrines leaves without acknowledging the answer, which presumably reflects his haste. Daos may wait until he has left the stage before delivering his lament to Tyche, which is clearly full of irony for the audience in view of the recent prologue and its speaker. Once again the slave uses the language of tragedy to express his emotion,[14] and the depth of his grief explains why he makes no announcement of the cook's arrival (216), being too engrossed in his own thoughts.

216. *Enter* COOK *and mute* ASSISTANT (222) *from* CHAIRESTRATOS' *house*
The cook explains his reasons for entry at once: his contract (presumably for the wedding of Chaireas and the girl (cf. 136–7) is now cancelled because of the news. He is unannounced, and this together with his obvious indignation would make his entrance sudden and surprising: its effect is primarily comic[15] and it provides a view of the bad news which contrasts amusingly with the grief of the household;[16] his loud speech is juxtaposed with Daos' emotional soliloquy and provokes a horrified reaction from the slave at such inappropriate

[13] See B(3) above.
[14] Austin (1970) ad loc. cites parallels from Sophokles and Euripides.
[15] Cf. Goldberg (1980) 35–6.
[16] Cf. Handley (1970) 14–15.

action at a time of mourning. This contributes to the progresssion of mood in the first act from the deeply serious beginning to the almost farcical ending where the cook and waiter enter in quick succession to bandy words with Daos[17] (see also GS ad loc.).

233a. *Exeunt* COOK *and* ASSISTANT, *presumably to the city*
The departure of the cook and his assistant is not explicit, but the evidence is against their remaining until the end of the act. Although the text 235b–237a is lacunose and the lost section is unclear, the rest of the act shows no evidence of the cook's presence: ὑμῶν (234) is unlikely to be addressed to him and his assistant since in addition to the absence of any response such an interpretation would deprive κοπτόμενοϲ of its comic force which is derived from a play on the double meaning (as often in New Comedy), a force it would retain if addressed back to the household; cf. CS ad loc. The sarcastic reference to the waiter in 232–3 would provide an effective exit-line.

233b. *Enter the* WAITER *from* CHAIRESTRATOS' *house*
The entrance is unannounced but implicitly prepared by the cook's parting comment (232–3) which identifies the waiter for the audience as he emerges speaking back with a pun (see above). He addresses the household[18] and his words again convey the state of grief inside as did Daos' at 164ff.: as with the cook's entrance, this arrival is primarily for comic effect; again Daos is horrified and orders the new entrant to move off (235, cf. 221).

246. *Exit the* WAITER *to the city*
The entrances and exits of the cook and waiter create a flurry of action at the end of the act which introduces a new element of comedy into scenes which had been primarily serious. The technique by which this is done is not uncommon in Menander: Handley (1970) 11 remarks: 'the pattern of introducing a new development towards the end of an act is a recurrent one in Menander and naturally enough the development is often sought by the arrival of a character new to the play or at least to the preceding sequence'.

245. DAOS [*to* WAITER]. Clear off away from our door! [*Exit* WAITER *to the city*] Now I see another mob approaching, of drunken men.

[17] Cf. A. G. Katsouris, *LCM* 8.2 (1983), 30–1.
[18] Cf. Austin (1970) ad loc.

[*Addresses them*] You've got sense. The role of fortune is unclear: be happy while there's time!

[*Exit* DAOS *to* CHAIRESTRATOS' *house*

Daos, left alone on stage, announces the approach of the chorus to perform in the act-break. The chorus in Menander appears to have been announced at the end of the first act only and was uninvolved in the action of play: its sole function was to provide a musical interlude,[19] and when introducing it characters use certain recurrent verbal formulae.[20] Daos' announcement is unusual in that it is the only certain example of a character directly addressing the chorus, who are usually referred to at a distance as 'some mob' although there may be another instance at Alexis fr. 107 Kock. Here they are congratulated on their sense (choruses being traditionally drunk) and encouraged in their celebrations (248–9). The point of breaking with what appears to have been convention may be to illustrate Daos' depression: the audience is assured of a happy ending by the prologue and has witnessed the comedy of the cook and the waiter, but Daos is distressed and praises those who enjoy themselves while they can (249). The address to the chorus highlights the gulf between the slave's perception of his plight and reality as the audience knows it: the act finishes with an ironic reference to τύχη ('chance'), whose divine personification has just delivered the prologue.

XOPOY

250. *Enter* SMIKRINES, CHAIRESTRATOS, *and* CHAIREAS *from the market-place*

Smikrines had left earlier to seek the male members of Kleostratos' family (213), and he now returns in mid-conversation with Chairestratos, as his first word, the resumptive particle εἶἑν, indicates: the stage their conversation has reached (arrangements for the burial) shows that the news of the supposed death has been passed on. This method of entry plunging straight into the dialogue is used to satisfy at once the audience's curiosity over the progression of Smikrines' plan, a curiosity engendered just before the act-break. Smikrines' reaction to the mention of the burial further characterizes his greed in contrast

[19] See generally Handley (1965) on *Dysk.* 230–2; cf. GS on *Epitr.* 169.
[20] Cf. W. G. Arnott, *ZPE* 31 (1978), 18–19.

to Chairestratos' sense of family responsibility: he is more concerned with securing the girl and hence the inheritance (252–6).

Chaireas does not speak until 284 but is almost certainly present from the beginning of the scene. GS ad loc. rebutt the earlier views which assigned a speaking role to Chaireas prior to 284; but the deictic ὁδί ('this fellow here', 262) suggests his presence (although it is not conclusive)[21] as does the state of his knowledge later in the scene: he has learnt of Kleostratos' 'death' (284) and of Smikrines' plan (297–8), and since he has up to now been in the market-place (213) and Daos has remained in Chairestratos' house, he can only have learnt the news from Smikrines, by entering with him and Chairestratos at 250; Smikrines would have had no reason to speak to him separately earlier.[22] Chaireas' silent presence in the scene also increases the emphasis on Smikrines' selfish disregard for others: Smikrines is now seen to make the proposal for marriage in front of the original prospective husband (253–4).

278a. *Exit* SMIKRINES *to his house*
Smikrines' exact exit-line is now lost, but the scene is building up to an angry departure as he rejects the idea of taking the property and leaving the girl. At 274 he contemptuously rejects Chairestratos' plea and leaves with some rejoinder after his brother has indicated his helplessness, thereby preventing any further discussion.

282–305. CHAIRESTRATOS [*in distraction*]. Let me be free of this life with all speed before I see what I never expected actually happening!

[*Staggers to his door and falls inside*

CHAIREAS. So! perhaps your misfortune, Kleostratos, deserves my pity and tears first, and mine second . . .

DAOS [*enters from* CHAIRESTRATOS' *house addressing his words back inside*]. Chairestratos, you are not behaving as you should! Stand up! This is no time to lose heart and lie down! [*Turns and sees* CHAIREAS] Chaireas, come and encourage him. Don't let him do it. All our fortunes are just about dependant on him. [*Turns back to door and addresses* CHAIRESTRATOS *again*] But come on, open the

[21] Cf. on *Perik.* 531 below (p. 96 n. 17).
[22] So Jacques (1978) 42.

door. Show yourself. Are you going to abandon your friends, Chairestratos, so shamefully?

Chairestratos' doors open and he is rolled out on the ekkyklema.

CHAIRESTRATOS. Daos, my boy, I'm struck down!

As the text stands there is no explicit indication that Chairestratos actually enters his house, but his continued presence would result in some dramatic awkwardness. The sight of Chairestratos collapsed before his door could only distract the audience's attention from Chaireas' emotional monologue[23] and create further difficulties over Daos' role at 299ff., where his words to Chairestratos do not favour the view that he enters and sees him for the first time on returning from abroad: rather, the absence of any element of greeting suggests that this is a continuing address which only now becomes audible.[24] Further, as Jacques[25] notes, if Chairestratos enters and collapses indoors, Daos enters to fetch help: if, however, he does see the stricken figure for the first time when he enters, the slave is deprived of motivation for his appearance. Chairestratos then departs not with a clear exit-line (although he may in the lacunose 278–80 have made his intentions plain), but with the despairing 282–3: the effect by which a clear exit-line is replaced by emotional words to emphasize the speaker's state of mind (here anger, grief, and hopelessness) is a favourite one in the extant Menander.[26]

Daos enters at 299 talking back to Chairestratos who is lying out of the audience's view behind the doors, encouraging him to get to his feet; for ἀνίϲταϲο ('stand up') in a faint scene cf. *Sik.* 363. GS ad loc. suggest that his words are heard from inside the house and that his call to Chaireas comes through the half-open door without the slave actually being seen by the audience: much more straightforward is for him to emerge, turn at 300 to see Chaireas, and call on him for help;

[23] Cf. ibid. 48–9; Goldberg (1980) 129 n. 10. Those critics who argue that he does remain on stage outside his door (D. Del Corno, *ZPE* 8 (1971), 29–32; Holzberg (1974) 31 n. 99; Katsouris (1975) 108 n. 2) cite as parallel technique the faints of Hekabe in Eur. *Hek.* 438ff. and of Iolaos in *Herakl.* 607–8, where in both cases the characters remain on stage motionless during a choral song before discovery by a new entrant. However, in the tragic passages the audience's attention is focused away from the stage containing the collapsed figure and on to the chorus in the orchestra, while on Menander's stage there is no corresponding physical separation of those involved which could prevent the slumped Chairestratos distracting the spectators from Chaireas' emotional monologue.

[24] Cf. Jacques (1978) 49.

[25] Ibid. 48.

[26] See C(5)(*a*) above.

the audience would assume that he has entered in a state of alarm to seek aid.

The slave's following words at 303–4 have been variously interpreted. Del Corno[27] believed them to constitute an order to Chairestratos, collapsed on-stage outside his door, to let his household see him, but this is ruled out by the difficulties of a collapse on stage discussed above; Austin (1970) ad loc. supposed the words to be addressed to Chaireas, who is urged to let Chairestratos within see him. The suggestion, made originally by Jacques (1978) 51–2,[28] that Daos' order in fact serves to introduce an entrance on the *ekkyklema* deserves serious consideration: in its favour are the passages of fifth-century drama where a similar order provides the cue for the appearance of a stricken character on this device, for example, Soph. *Aj.* 344, where the chorus orders ἀλλ᾽ ἀνοίγετε ('But open up').[29] With Daos' order that Chairestratos be taken inside (387), which has caused some puzzlement,[30] Jacques (1978) 55 compares Ar. *Thesm.* 265 εἴϲω τιϲ ὡϲ τάχιϲτά μ᾽ εἰϲκυκληϲάτω ('someone roll me in with all speed'). In the light of this comparison he takes 387 as the cue for the *ekkyklema* to be rolled indoors where Daos orders εἴϲω τιϲ ἀγέτω τουτονί ('someone take him in'). If the suggestion is correct, this recognizably tragic device is used to stress Chairestratos' degree of collapse, and Daos' plan of a feigned illness is conceived from this spectacle of his master prostrate on the *ekkyklema*, adding irony to the slave's expression at 329–30.[31] Attractive though the suggestion is, there remain some problems: while orders to open the doors are indeed regular cues for such scenes in earlier drama, they are nowhere found addressed to the person actually on the device, as here (note ἄνοιγε singular and specific, as shown by the closely connected φανερὸν πόει | ϲαυτόν) but rather to others, usually undefined attendants.[32] Further, the order at 387 is inconclusive evidence since at *Kith.* 51 a virtually identical order is used apparently to summon a slave from within to take some articles into the house (see note ad loc.), and it may simply be that a slave helps Chairestratos off the stage

[27] *ZPE* 6 (1970), 216–17.

[28] See also S. Halliwell, *LCM* 8.2 (1983), 31–2.

[29] Further examples collected by Jacques (1978) 53–5; in more detail by Halliwell (op. cit., n. 30); see also W. S. Barrett, *Hippolytos* (Oxford, 1964) on 808.

[30] 'Why should Chairestratos need taking into his own home? I can only suggest that he is already beginning to act the part of a sick man' (GS ad loc.).

[31] Cf. Halliwell (op. cit., n. 30) 32.

[32] See e.g. R. Jebb on Soph. *Aj.* 344.

here. Accordingly the case for the *ekkyklema* remains unproven, and other suggestions for the staging are equally deserving of attention; GS ad loc. suggest that Chairestratos is helped off by Daos, Arnott (1979) by attendant slaves.

379. *Exit* CHAIREAS *to the city*
Chaireas leaves to fetch an accomplice to play the doctor (376 ff.). The Bodmer papyrus assigns 383 to him, but this leaves him no obvious point at which he can leave before the end of the act, unless Austin (1969) is correct to assign 387–9 to him as well. However, an exit at 379, with Daos' words ταχὺ μὲν οὖν ('yes, and be quick about it!') speeding him on his way, appears most likely: in his haste he does not even acknowledge the slave's encouragement. This exit and that of Chairestratos at 387 create the flurry of action not uncommon at Menandrean act-endings (cf. on 246 above) as characters depart with their orders: in addition an air of positive activity is created which forms a marked contrast with the air of gloom and hopelessness earlier in the scene. These effects would be considerably diminished if Chaireas were to remain until the end of the scene: it is worth noting that Menander has not felt obliged to make explicit in the characters' words action which would have been obvious in performance.

387. *Exit* CHAIRESTRATOS *to his house*

390. *Exit* DAOS *to* CHAIRESTRATOS' *house*
Daos leaves in a spirit of hope, looking forward to the sport and contest to come (388–9): these lines are probably to be viewed as soliloquy rather than an address to Chairestratos, who in that case would remain on stage to accompany Daos in at 390; Blundell (1980) 51 compares the short exit monologues at *Epitr.* 416–18 and *Sam.* 614.

ΧΟΡΟΥ

391. *Enter* SMIKRINES *from his house*
In his entrance monologue Smikrines reveals his anger over Daos' failure to bring an inventory of the property (cf. 274–5): the audience would perhaps assume that he is coming to find the slave, although this is not made explicit, and their interest in seeing the deception begin would make the old man's appearance acceptable even without any clear motivation. Before his meeting with Daos, Smikrines' greed is again emphasized: he can now drop any pretence of a polite approach and act solely in his own interest (394–6).

399. *Enter* DAOS *from* CHAIRESTRATOS' *house*

Smikrines delivers an implicit announcement of Daos (398) which is full of unintentional irony: his confident claim to know the slave's tricks is followed at once by Daos' entrance beginning the intrigue which takes in the old man completely. The slave bursts on to the stage and a farcical scene follows as he quotes tragedy and rushes up and down (410) ignoring Smikrines. The scene recalls in some respects *Mis.* 284ff., where Getas is genuinely unaware of Kleinias' presence (323–4): here of course Daos knows perfectly well that Smikrines is there, as shown by the sudden address at 419.

It is not clear from the text how Daos knows his victim is on stage, and W. S. Anderson[33] suggests that he enters during the last part of Smikrines' monologue and is seen to notice the old man and choose his moment to appear to enter. However, Bain (1977) 175–7[34] argues convincingly that this is a type-scene which the audience would recognize as such and so would accept the lack of motivation and explanation for the entrance. The dramatic short cut involved produces an abrupt and comic beginning to the scene, and since the audience is eager to see the intrigue in action, and Smikrines discomfited, Daos' unexplained appearance would not unduly tax their credibility.

430. *Enter* CHAIREAS, *the* FALSE DOCTOR, *and his* ASSISTANT (cf. 455) *from the city*

The group enters just as Daos has revealed to Smikrines that Chaireas has gone to fetch a doctor (429–30): this implicit announcement leads straight into a visual announcement (430) which allows Daos to address the 'doctor' at once and hurry him indoors without the need to introduce him to Smikrines: this all contributes to the effect of swift action and the rapid progress of the intrigue.

431. *Exeunt* FALSE DOCTOR, ASSISTANT, *and* CHAIREAS *to* CHAIRESTRATOS' *house*

Daos urges the 'doctor' to hurry indoors (431): he makes some brief reply, now lost, and leaves the stage. Under the constraints of the three-actor rule Chaireas is played in this scene by a mute, and a swift departure alleviates any awkwardness in his enforced silence, as he leaves before having a chance to speak.

[33] *Phoenix*, 24 (1970), 233 n. 12.

[34] Note especially p. 176: 'We are not supposed to wonder how Daos knows to choose his moment so well'.

432. *Exit* DAOS *to* CHAIRESTRATOS' *house*

There is no sign that the slave is present during the meeting of Smikrines and the 'doctor' which begins at 439, and the next words certainly attributable to him are 467b; as Blundell (1980) 26–7 remarks, Smikrines' monologue (433 ff.) is better spoken in solitude than in the silent presence of Daos. Most probably, then, he leaves at 432, sweeping off in mock-grief with his quotation of Eur. *Or.* 232 providing the exit-line[35] as he follows the 'doctor' inside.

By the time the papyrus resumes at 439, the 'doctor' and his assistant have reappeared from Chairestratos' house and are in conversation with Smikrines.

464. *Exeunt* FALSE DOCTOR *and* ASSISTANT *to the city*

The 'doctor' leaves, apparently hinting darkly to Smikrines that he may have some fatal disease (462–4), his departure fulfilling his earlier attempts to leave (455) when Smikrines delayed his exit. As often the device of delayed exit is used to introduce an important scene,[36] and here its use shows that Smikrines is convinced of the 'doctor's' identity and wants to be sure of Chairestratos' imminent death.

Bain (1977) 107 n. 3 suggests that δ]εῦρ' ἀπὸ τῆc θύραc ἔτι ('over here, further away from the door', 457) indicates that the 'doctor' has moved back towards the door with the intention of re-entering the house. However at *Mis.* 429 and *Sam.* 304 virtually identical phrases are found whose function is purely to introduce movement away from the door prior to private dialogue, and that is probably the case here too; cf. Blume (1974) 106.

465. *Enter* DAOS *from* CHAIRESTRATOS' *house*

Daos speaks at 467b for the first time since 432, which probably constituted his exit-line (see above). Θορυβήcω τουτονί ('I'll confuse him') is clearly an aside, and the marginal note in the papyrus, ηcυχη, is in this case correctly applied (cf. on 94a above). Smikrines appears to believe that he is alone on stage when the false doctor and his assistant leave, as his words 465–467a read like soliloquy; cf. Bain (1977) 106–8. Daos must then reappear at some time after 465, and Bain (op. cit.) argues convincingly that the scene is best played if Daos is seen to overhear 465 ff., the lines in which Smikrines reveals his anxiety: the slave's aside (467b) will indicate his intention to exploit

[35] See C(5)(*a*) above.
[36] See C(4) above.

these very fears. An entrance actually at 467b, while not being unintelligible, would lose this effect. At 468 the fragmentary line may preserve the beginning of a feigned entrance monologue with the intention of deceiving Smikrines further; cf. Bain (1977) 108.

[ΧΟΡΟΥ]

491. *Enter* KLEOSTRATOS, *presumably from the harbour*
The papyrus is defective at this point and the first intelligible action comes at 491 where the traditional greeting on homecoming appears to be delivered as a soliloquy; the earlier speakers in the fragmentary lines up to 490 must now have left the stage.

506. *Enter* DAOS *from* CHAIRESTRATOS' *house*
Kleostratos resolves to knock at 499, where his choice of verb, παίειν instead of the more usual κόπτειν, may reflect his enthusiasm.[37] The emergence of Daos to answer the door is suggested and prepared by Kleostratos' immediate concern for the safety of his faithful slave (497–8). Daos responds in the gap at 499[38]—as the door-knocking scene is non-comic it is swiftly over[39]—yet fails, apparently, to recognize his master until 506, keeping up the story that Chairestratos is dead and that the mourners are not to be troubled. This is best explained by supposing the door to remain firmly unopened (so GS and Arnott (1979) ad loc.): Daos is naturally reluctant to open it and risk the true state of affairs indoors being discovered (cf. 383–6 on the need to involve as few people as possible).[40] At 506 the recognition takes place (for the oath (506) and ἔχω cε ('I have you', 508) compare the recognition scene at *Mis.* 210ff.); probably the door is opened at 504, where ἄν[οιγε ('open up') can be restored, as Daos enters to drive away the troublesome caller; and the master and his slave come face to face at 506.

[37] See B(5)(*a*) n. 66 above.

[38] Austin (1970) suggests τίϲ τὴν θύραν as Daos' response, comparing the phrase at Herod. i. 3. Compare also *CGF* 368. 5–6 (*adespoton* of New Comedy): κόψω δὲ κ[| τίϲ τὴν θύ[ραν.

[39] See B(5)(*a*) above.

[40] Austin (1970) proposes that Daos does not open the door at 499, but in such a way that he sees neither his master nor his slave. This seems unnecessarily complicated, since voices from behind the door could be heard on-stage; see the examples listed by GS on *Aspis* 299.

2

Georgos

21. *Exit young man, probably to his house*

The youth leaves with the express purpose of devising some way to avoid the marriage which is being arranged for him (20–1).[1] His direction of exit is not explicit, but he is unlikely to leave to the city, since it is from that side that the two women enter (22), and an exit towards the country is improbable as Gorgias, brother of the pregnant girl, whom the youth has no wish to meet, may be working there (18–19).[2] It is worth noting that the action of 24ff., where Philinna is restrained from calling the youth out to denounce him (falsely) as an ἀλαζών ('charlatan'), would lose much of its impact if the audience knew he was not at home.

On departure the youth leaves the impression of a well-meaning yet weak-willed character: he is loyal to Myrrhine's daughter (15–16) and determined to avoid marriage to his stepsister, yet is too nervous to knock on his beloved's door and explain his position (17).[3] The location of this speech in the opening scenes deserves attention:[4] Holzberg (1974) 46 points out that its almost exclusively expository nature (as far as it survives), and the absence of proper names are features typical of prologue speeches in Menander; in view of the proximity of the choral break and the probable amount of text missing from the start of the play,[5] the youth's speech may have been preceded by some opening scene, e.g. a divine prologue (so Webster (1974) 142–3) or a dialogue scene (so Holzberg (1974) 47). A further possibility is that the play began with the youth already on stage, unable to knock at his beloved's door; note ὀκνῶ πάλαι ('I've been too scared for ages', 17), and on opening tableaux see on *Mis.* A1.

[1] Cf. the exit of Moschion at *Sam.* 94–5.

[2] So K. Dziatzko, *RhM* 54 (1899), 507 n. 1.

[3] Blundell (1980) 49 points out the humour of the weak lover's inability to knock at the door here and at *Dysk.* 267–8; cf. Ter. *Ad.* 633.

[4] In what follows it is assumed, in view of the prologue-type features of the youth's speech, that the surviving fragment is from the first, not the second, act; for an examination of the inconclusive evidence on this point see W. G. Arnott, *ZPE* 31 (1978), 16–19.

[5] See Arnott, op. cit. 16–17.

22. *Enter* MYRRHINE *and* PHILINNA *from the city*
The couple enter in mid-conversation, as is made clear by the connective ἀλλά and the explicit reference to the story imagined to have been related prior to entry (22–4). As Dziatzko suggests,[6] Myrrhine has probably fetched Philinna from the city, and has related the circumstances to her; an entrance from Myrrhine's house is ruled out by Philinna's ignorance until 87 of the advanced state of the girl's pregnancy.

The effect of this entrance lies in its juxtaposition with the young man's exit, having declared himself loyal to Myrrhine's daughter and in considerable distress at what has happened: he is now subject to abuse and accusations of treachery (τὸν ἀλαζόνα 'the charlatan', 26–7; ὁ μιαρὸϲ οὗτοϲ 'this rogue', 30). The technique by which one character's declaration of a view or attitude is at once followed by the appearance of another whose words completely contradict that declaration is not uncommon in Menander (cf. *Aspis* 398–9; *Mis.* 258 with notes ad loc.).

At 27–8 Philinna makes a movement towards the youth's door, and is restrained by Myrrhine (28a): this delays the women from entering Myrrhine's house at once and keeps them on stage until Daos arrives; cf. GS on 22–41.

31b–4. MYRRHINE. His servant Daos approaches from the farm. Let's move a little out of the way.
PHILINNA [*staying firmly on the spot*]. Tell me, what do we care for him?
MYRRHINE [*firmly drawing her away from centre-stage*]. Really it would be best.

Myrrhine makes a visual announcement (31–2) and the two women stand back to listen.[7] According to the *OCT*, when Myrrhine urges moving out of the way, Philinna objects (33–4) and uses the phrase καλόν γ' ἂν εἴη ironically, as it is used at Xenarchos 8K, the only other surviving instance; see GS ad loc. However, this implies that the old woman does not withdraw, which is unlikely, since Daos does not see the couple until 41, unless Myrrhine is imagined to overrule her

[6] Op. cit. 509; cf. GS on 22.

[7] For entrance announcement followed by withdrawal to eavesdrop cf. *Dysk.* 148; *Perik.* 368; *Sam.* 368. The device is adopted from fifth-century tragedy (e.g. Aesch. *Cho.* 20–1; Eur. *El.* 107–8, *Ion* 76–7; Soph. *OK* 113–14: see Leo (1908) 68; E. Fraenkel, *Beobachtungen zur Aristophanes* (Rome, 1962), 22–3.

and pull her back in a dumb show before Daos arrives. This latter solution seems over-complicated, and Arnott[8] is surely correct to assign 34b to Myrrhine, so that the nurse is firmly and explicitly overruled and drawn back before Daos appears.

The two slaves enter from the country, an area whose importance has been explained in the young man's speech: it is where Gorgias, the pregnant girl's brother, is working (4, 18). Both the visual announcement and Daos' first words pick up this emphasis ἐξ ἀγροῦ (32), ἀγρόν (35). Arnott[9] argues in favour of the restoration ὄζουϲ ('branches', 32) as the description of the objects that Syros takes indoors at 39–40, and if this is correct, the arrival of the slaves carrying branches, decoration for a wedding ceremony, would provide a vivid answer to Philinna's question of 29–30 by confirming that the youth's marriage to his stepsister is imminent. Daos enters with a monologue full of joy and confidence over the news he is sure will be welcome, and his mood contrasts with the gloom and despair shown by Myrrhine. The immediate effect of his words is, however, puzzlement as, after so much talk of marriage (21, 29) and the obvious significance of the branches he is carrying, he enters praising the quality of the farmland (the significance of this only becomes clear later): Blundell (1980) 46 notes that to puzzle the audience at the start of a monologue is a frequent device in Menander to arouse interest.

40. *Exit* SYROS *to the young man's house*
Syros leaves under orders from Daos who may make a movement to send him in which causes him to catch sight of the women; so Arnott (1979) ad loc.

84a. *Exit* DAOS *to the young man's house*
Daos leaves as soon as he has delivered his speech, without waiting to hear Myrrhine's reaction. The end of his speech shows signs of elevated expression with tragic metre and grandiose vocabulary, and the high-flown tone is maintained by the gnomic statement rounding off the speech (81–2; cf. GS ad loc.). The slave's abrupt exit may be intended to indicate enthusiasm for the news he is bringing: so deep is his conviction that it is welcome that he feels no need to wait for confirmation. As the audience knows, this is exceptionally bad news

[8] Op. cit. 22–3: he remarks that the example from Xenarchos does not exclude a non-ironical sense for the phrase.

[9] Op. cit. 21–2.

from the women's point of view, despite Daos' high spirits (ὦ χαῖρε πολλά ('a very good day to you!') picked up by ἔρρωσο πολλά ('a very goodbye to you!')), and Myrrhine's καὶ σύ ('and to you too', 54) is a stunned response: at 85a she gives visible evidence of her anxiety by walking up and down wringing her hands.

3

Dis Exapaton

14–18. MOSCHOS' FATHER. Let us go, Lydos.

LYDOS. But if you left me here too . . .

MOSCHOS' FATHER [*moving to go*]. Let us go. He'll suffice.

LYDOS [*reluctant to leave*]. Deal with him harshly, Sostratos, goad the reprobate. He is disgracing all of us, his friends.

SOSTRATOS [*sarcastically, when they are out of earshot*]. Gone already, has he?

[*Exeunt Lydos and Moschos' father to the city*[1]

Lydos' reluctance to leave is only overruled when the order to go is repeated and the resulting delay in the exit is used to characterize him by revealing his eagerness to chastise Moschos personally; cf. the scene at *Sik.* 146–7. The original effect of the exit can be recovered by comparison with the plot as it is known from Plautus' adaptation, *Bacchides*; as Moschos is innocent of any treachery, there is considerable irony when Lydos leaves encouraging Sostratos to rebuke his friend severely.[2]

Sostratos remains on-stage with a monologue revealing uncertainty and a conflict of emotions between anger and loyalty towards his friend (cf. Blundell (1980) 67). Critics have disagreed over the interpretation of his opening words, a difficulty left unresolved by comparison with Plautus' version (*Bacch.* 500–1), where the monologue spoken by Mnesilochus is too far removed from that of Sostratos in Menander to allow any conclusions on how Plautus interpreted the Greek. GS, pointing out that τούτου (19) refers to Moschos and suggesting that φροῦδοϲ will have an elevated meaning (as is common in tragedy) takes the phrase to mean 'He [Moschos] has already gone for good'[3] (that is, to perdition); however Bain (1979) 206

[1] The direction of the exit can be deduced from the corresponding exit in Plautus' adaptation *Bacchides*, assuming, as the extant Greek suggests, that he has preserved the basic structure of his original. Lydus and Philoxenus, the corresponding characters, enter at 405 from the city and presumably return home there at 498.

[2] For the effect compare *Geo.* 22ff., the women's condemnation of the sincere and despairing youth.

[3] Cf. Arnott (1979) ad loc.: 'Too late, he's come to grief'.

n. 51 points out that at *Dysk.* 776 φροῦδοι . . . εἰcί is found with the straightforward meaning 'they've gone', and his proposal to take Lydos as the subject results in a sarcastic exit acknowledgement[4] and provides a more satisfactory interpretation which is adopted in the above version.

After 30. *Enter* SOSTRATOS' *father*[5]

Discussion on this entrance is hindered by the loss of 31–46. Handley[6] prints as 30b [ἀλλ' ὁρῶ γὰ]ρ̣ τ̣[ουτο]ν̣ί: the *OCT* leaves the latter half of the line blank. A visual announcement such as that restored by Handley would be entirely plausible: for the expression ἀλλά . . . γάρ and a deictic pronoun, regularly found in visual announcements in fifth-century tragedy,[7] cf. *Dysk.* 607; *Sam.* 280, 639.

63. *Exeunt* SOSTRATOS *and his* FATHER

Sostratos instructs his father to disregard for the moment the lies he has been told by the slave Syros and to follow him off, using a brisk series of imperatives which reflect his determination to act and be avenged on his (as he believes) faithless sweetheart (59): this contrasts strongly with his wavering attitudes in 18ff. and is ironical as it is based on a false impression of Moschos' relationship with her. The exit is delayed by his father's incredulous reaction (60) and the orders have to be repeated: the delay is used to characterize the father who, when he is convinced he will get the money, follows enthusiastically. GS ad loc. comment on the dramatic importance of an unsympathetic portrayal of the old man whose chief concern is for the money, and who will later be cheated of it. The technique of the delayed exit for characterization is in some respects comparable to that at 14–15.

The direction of the exit is irrecoverable: it may be to the father's house or, as GS on 59 suggest, to the town.

[4] Cf. E. W. Handley, *Menander and Plautus: a Study in Comparison* (London, 1968), 11: 'So he's gone then?'.

[5] Returning from the city? Cf. Pl. *Bacch.* 347–8 ('Nicobulus'' last appearance, departing to the forum).

[6] Op. cit. 22.

[7] Cf. J. D. Denniston, *The Greek Particles*[2] (Oxford, 1954), 103; T. B. L. Webster, *CR* 47 (1933), 119. Note also the *adespoton* of New Comedy *CGF* 255: ἀλλ' εἰc]ορῶ γὰρ τουτονὶ τόν δεcπότη[ν ('but I see my master here'). Phrases based on ἀλλ' εἰcορω γὰρ τόνδε were far from uncommon in fifth-century drama (see J. Diggle, *ZPE* 24 (1977), 291–4), and this may have influenced the technique of New Comedy.

ΧΟΡΟΥ

[*Re-enter* SOSTRATOS *and his* FATHER]

90. *Exit* SOSTRATOS' *father to the city*
Sostratos' father gives his general motivation explicitly (89–90), although the details of his mission are now lost. He reaffirms Sostratos' task, to reprove his friend (90), and in a clear echo of the final scenes of the last act Sostratos is left alone on stage as a departing character exhorts him to chastise Moschos. His monologue picks up his speech of 18ff. by verbal echoes which are examined by Blundell (1980) 33 n. 14; Handley (1970) 17–18 remarks on the methods of linking and transition over the act-break by means of the two scenes of Sostratos and his father which flank the interlude.

102. *Enter* MOSCHOS *from the* HETAERA'*s house*
Moschos enters without an explicit announcement, but implicitly announced by Sostratos who is pondering his friend's role in the supposed treachery (98–9). His words on entry convey at once his motivation: he is looking for Sostratos (ποῦ γῆϲ ἐϲτί; ('where on earth is he?', 103), a phrase which recurs elsewhere, with modifications, in similar situations.)[8] The manner in which 102b–3a are delivered is however unclear, and it is not at once obvious whether they are spoken back to someone, presumably the hetaera, inside the house[9] or whether they are spoken to no particular addressee as an expression of Moschos' private thoughts.[10] At face value the words are ambiguous, but since the examples of ποῦ ἐϲτί in entrances in search of someone at *Dysk.* 588 and *Epitr.* 442 are certainly found in monologue form, it is tempting to assume that the unclear examples here and at *Sam.* 690 were also delivered in that way.[11] It is interesting, but nothing more, to note that in his adaptation (*Bacch.* 526) Plautus took the words as an address back into the house, and made his interpretation explicit by using the vocative 'Bacchis'.[12]

[8] Note that Plautus' version (*Bacch.* 526–9) contains no corresponding 'ubi est'; on the phrase in Menander and equivalent expression in Roman Comedy see B(4) in the first part of this book.

[9] So Handley, op. cit. 17; Arnott (1979) ad loc.

[10] So GS on 102.

[11] See B(4) above.

[12] Cf. Bain (1979) 25–6.

4
Dyskolos

1. *Enter* PAN *from his shrine*

49. *Exit* PAN *to his shrine*

Pan uses the approach of Chaireas and Sostratos as his reason for departure after delivery of his prologue; on the conventional form of the announcement with καὶ γάϱ see Handley (1965) ad loc. and compare 232.

50. *Enter* CHAIREAS *and* SOSTRATOS *from the right*[1]
Pan has identified the new arrivals and related the background in his prologue, which enables them to enter in mid-conversation[2] and avoid repeating material to the audience. Chaireas delivers an apistetic question τί φῄϲ ('what's that you're saying?') and summarizes what he is imagined to have been just told (50–2a); for a similar technique cf. *Mis.* 259–60. His first words bring explicit confirmation of Pan's prologue by reference to the girl's care for the nymph's statues (51, cf. 36–9).

81. *Enter* PYRRHIAS *from the left*
The entrance of the running slave was a standard scene in Greek Comedy,[3] and Handley (1965) ad loc. notes how Menander is careful to individualize this entrance with two comic elements: that Pyrrhias who was depicted as a hunter (71) is now being pursued (82), and that he stubs his toe (91–2). The slave is not explicitly announced, which makes his sudden arrival abrupt, but is expected from 78 as Sostratos wonders at his lateness: this preparation enables the scene of his arrival to be unhampered by identification and explanation; GS ad loc. compare the arrival of Kreon at Soph. *OT* 289–90.[4] Above all, this

[1] For the significance of the wing entrances in this play which is, untypically, set in the country, not the city, see Handley (1965) 129; in the following stage directions, 'left' means to the farms of Gorgias and Knemon, 'right' to Kallippides' estate and to the city.

[2] The manner of entry may provide support for the restoration of the ed. princ. in 49 ϲ[υγκοινουμ]ένουϲ; see GS on 48–9.

[3] E.g. Ar. *Av.* 1122–3; *CGF* 239 (*adespoton* of New Comedy). See further, and for a short bibliography, W. S. Anderson, *Phoenix*, 24 (1970), 230–1.

[4] See further B(7) in the first part of this book.

terrified entrance serves to begin the build-up to Knemon's arrival at 153 by portraying him as a dreadful monster; the speed of the broken lines (82–3), the assertion of madness (82a), and Pyrrhias' obvious distress all contribute to this effect.

134. *Exit* CHAIREAS *to the right*
The major reasons for supposing Chaireas to depart now are given by GS on 135, to which there is little to add. His words do not make his movements explicit, but the omission of a clear exit-line is not frequent in Menander[5] and here the effect is of a hasty retreat as Knemon approaches, a comic turn of events following Chaireas' confident self-eulogy (57b ff.).

144. *Exit* PYRRHIAS *to the right*
Pyrrhias leaves with a clear exit-line announcing Knemon (143–4), and Sostratos is left alone on stage, deserted by his helpers, to face him. GS on 142–6 suggest that Pyrrhias addresses ὑπάγω, βέλτιϲτε ('I'm off, sir', 146) to Knemon as he leaves, as there is no parallel in New Comedy for a slave using this term to his master. However, it seems unlikely that the terrified Pyrrhias would address Knemon before leaving, and the explanation of Handley (1965) ad loc. that Pyrrhias may use this form of address to Sostratos as he is a companion rather than an ordinary slave, seems preferable.

153. *Enter* KNEMON *from the left*
The audience's anticipation of Knemon's appearance has been built up since Pyrrhias' entrance (81) and his actual arrival has been awaited since the announcement of 143. The tension is increased as his appearance is delayed for up to eight lines (145–53) as Sostratos expresses his fear in his monologue and describes the old man's fearsome approach (147–50).[6] It is unclear at exactly which point during Sostratos' monologue Knemon becomes visible to the audience, but in the interests of increasing the suspense it will presumably be as late as possible, and certainly not as early as 145 as Arnott (1979) ad loc. supposes.

In the course of these elaborate preparations for Knemon's entrance, the audience would no doubt overlook the fact that it is unmotivated: as GS on 189 remark, he is not pursuing Pyrrhias, and

[5] See C(5) above.
[6] Cf. GS on 153; Blundell (1980) 45.

his household (as subsequent events show) is not expecting him home yet.

Knemon's first words baffle the audience, as instead of the expected fulminations against those who disturb him, he enters professing envy of Perseus (for this device at the start of a monologue cf. *Geo.* 35 and note); it subsequently emerges that this is in fact further illustration of Knemon's antisocial character, as he too would like to turn men to stone.[7] With οἴμοι ('oh no!', 167) Knemon catches sight of Sostratos who has withdrawn to stand by his door.[8]

178. *Exit* KNEMON *to his house*

Knemon has no explicit exit-line, but Sostratos' monologue (179ff.) shows that he is now alone on stage. Knemon's parting words (177b–8) are given prominence by their position, and emphasize his unapproachable nature;[9] cf. his exit-line at 515. The papyrus has a dicolon after ϲυνέδριον (177) which the ed. princ. interpreted as evidence of a change of speaker, assigning 177b–8 to Sostratos as the opening to his monologue; however, as the papyrus explicitly gives 179 to Sostratos by name, the dicolon is more likely to signify a change of addressee, as Knemon stops speaking to Sostratos and leaves with an expression of his personal feelings.[10]

189. *Enter* KNEMON'*s daughter from* KNEMON'*s house*

The girl is given a door announcement (188) where the choice of verb πλήϲϲειν is probably intended to suggest a hasty entrance.[11] At 182b Sostratos starts to move off towards the city, having resolved to fetch help: the door noise delays his exit and as often the interrupted movement introduces an important scene, here of Sostratos' first contact with his beloved.[12] The announcement focuses attention on the door where the girl enters with her lament (189) whose strict metre and elevated language are vividly tragic and introduce a fresh serious tone; Handley (1965) ad loc. remarks that the water-jug which the girl carries (200) might recall the lamenting appearance of the heroine in

7 The evidence of this mythological comparison forms a major part of the challenge of N. Zagagi, *Tradition and Originality in Plautus* (Göttingen, 1980), 29–30, to the arguments of Fraenkel (1922) 8ff. for a wholly Plautine origin for the mythological comparisons at the start of monologues in his adaptations.

8 For similar withdrawals cf. *Geo.* 35 and note.

9 For the effect see C(5) above.

10 For a similar use of the dicolon see *Epitr.* 1120.

11 See B(2) above.

12 See for further examples C(4) above.

Eur. *Elek.* 77–8. Both presentation and form contribute to the impact of this entrance.

203. *Exit* SOSTRATOS *to the shrine*
Sostratos' lack of a clear exit-line throws emphasis on his parting words, and this is used to highlight the irony in his invocation and rhetorical question (202–3); having heard the prologue, the audience knows his infatuation is caused by Pan.

206. *Enter* DAOS *from* GORGIAS' *house*
As Sostratos departs into the shrine, the creaking door heralds the arrival of Daos: since the girl can mistake it for the noise of Knemon's door, she must by now have moved towards the centre of the stage, and goes back to Knemon's door after 206 when she realizes who is the actual entrant; as GS ad loc. remark, she cannot speak 205–6b while running back to her door. Daos enters speaking back to Gorgias' mother (ϲοι 'for you', 206) which both provides his motivation—he has been there too long and must go to help Gorgias—and explains his failure to notice the girl at once, since his attention is directed back into the house.

211. *Enter* SOSTRATOS *from the shrine*
Sostratos emerges with the water-jug, and the circumstances of his opening address are not wholly clear: GS ad loc. are probably correct to suggest that he enters with λάμβανε | τηνδί ('here, take this') but finds the girl has moved, and she then calls him over to her door. Clearly the girl knows Daos is watching since she delivered the door announcement (203–4) which heralded his appearance on stage, and her abrupt φέρε δεῦρο ('bring it over here') and exit with no word of thanks may reflect her embarrassment at being seen in contact with a strange young man. Sostratos fails to see Daos, being too engrossed in his infatuation: having addressed his good wishes to the girl as she leaves (213) he turns to emotional self-apostrophe.[13]

[13] For examples of self-address in lovers' monologues see Blundell (1980) 66–7. Handley (1965) assigns 214b–15a to Pyrrhias, supposing him to have fled at 144 into the shrine: the resulting difficulty over the swift change required of the actor playing the girl from her exit at 212 to reappear as Pyrrhias at 214 may be remedied by an extra appearing as the girl at the door at 212 while the actor speaks φέρε δεῦρο from within while changing costumes; similar schemes are proposed by J. G. Griffith, *CQ* 10 (1960), 113–17; Webster (1960) 225–6. However, the need for such complicated action is removed once 214b is recognized as self-address, as Webster, *CR* 15 (1965), 17–18 subsequently realized; Pyrrhias leaves at 144 and takes no further part in the act (cf. Goldberg (1980) 136 n. 6).

212. *Exit* GIRL *to* KNEMON'*s house*

218. *Exit* SOSTRATOS *to the right*
Sostratos leaves on his original mission of 181–2 to fetch Getas (216–17), failing to see Daos or hear his remarks.

232. *Exit* DAOS *to the left*
On entry at 206 Daos expressed the intention of finding Gorgias and helping him dig: his motivation has now changed (226–7), and he intends to tell the girl's brother what he has seen to save her from what he believes to be an attempt at seduction. His decision to leave at 229 has decidedly increased urgency and is highly ironic for the audience.

The approach of the chorus[14] is announced as appears to have been traditional at this point (cf. *Aspis* 246–7 and note) but its arrival is secondary to the speaker's decision to leave the stage: he is already resolved to go and the drunken chorus is mentioned as a reason for withdrawal more as a matter of convention (232 = *Epitr.* 171) than genuine motivation; cf. *Epitr.* 171; *Perik.* 266.

ΧΟΡΟΥ

223. *Enter* GORGIAS *and* DAOS *from the left*
The couple enter in mid-conversation as is shown by the adversative particle δέ (233) which implies that Gorgias' words are in response to something prior to entry: the following brief reference to Daos' imagined report of events at once indicates to the audience both the topic of conversation, and how much has been reported to Gorgias (which, as often with this method of entry, avoids the repetition of detail known already to the audience).[15]

259. *Enter* SOSTRATOS *from the right*
Daos initiates a visual announcement when he abruptly calls attention to Sostratos with μικρὸν δ' ἐπιϲχεϲ ('but wait a moment', 255). Gorgias at once notices the newcomer's elegant clothing and assumes

[14] Πανιϲτάϲ (Lloyd-Jones) or Παιανιϲτάϲ (Handley, defending the papyrus reading)? Handley (1965) ad loc. acknowledges both the metrical arguments against the papyrus reading and the fact that the title is not attested in fourth-century Attica, but retains it in the absence of a decisive counter-argument; GS ad loc. prefer the metrical regularity of Lloyd-Jones' emendation and note that a group of 'Pan-worshippers' would be wholly appropriate given Pan's shrine on stage. The emended reading seems then preferable: scribal error in transcribing the word would be hardly surprising.

[15] See further B(6) above.

he is up to no good (258): his condemnation is amusing for the audience since they know Sostratos' intentions to be honourable. His entrance monologue at once gives his motivation for returning, having failed to find Getas (cf. *PGhôran* ii. 105–6) and his reference to his mother (260–1) prepares for the slave's appearance with the cook at the end of the act.

At 267–8 Sostratos states his intention to knock but his movement is delayed by Gorgias' address, the interrupted movement as often introducing an important scene;[16] cf. his delayed exit at 188.

378. *Exit* DAOS *to the left*

Daos delivers a clear exit-line (378) and his departure is well motivated (376–7): his diligence over his work recalls his first appearance (206–7) where he was keen to join Gorgias. He is also clearly weary of what he views as the charade of dressing up Sostratos (371–2).

381. *Exit* GORGIAS *to the left*

The movements from 381 are not explicit in the text, but may be deduced as follows. Sostratos' speech (381b ff.) has the appearance of a monologue,[17] and indeed Gorgias takes no further direct part in the scene after 381a. However, he has no explicit exit-line and there are no self-evident reasons why he should leave before Sostratos, since logically he should wait to accompany his new friend to the fields. The answer to the obscurity over Gorgias' whereabouts may lie in Menander's handling of his stage conventions: if the three-actor rule[18] did apply, GS 17 must be correct to suggest that the reason Daos and Gorgias leave before Sostratos is that the actor playing Daos would have to change costume to enter from the opposite wing at 393 in the role of Sikon, and the actor playing Gorgias would have to change to enter from that same wing in the role of Getas at 401: if Daos and Gorgias left with Sostratos, there would be no time to change costume and move from one wing to the other. Webster (1974) 83 goes further and argues that the actor playing Gorgias could leave with Sostratos at 392 and in the nine lines until 401 move from one wing to the other and change costume: on this interpretation Getas' comically late entry, which attracts specific comment (401–2), burdened with luggage, is a device to conceal this behind-the-scenes activity, since the slave cannot enter with the cook for the simple reason that the actor is not

[16] See further C(4) above.
[17] Cf. GS on 381; Blundell (1980) 80.
[18] On this see A(1) above.

yet available to assume the role. However, Webster's view fails to take account of the fact that on the evidence of Sostratos' speech (which is apparently a monologue) Gorgias is no longer present at 392; the most convenient point of exit remains unclear. Gorgias can hardly leave in silence at some point during the monologue as this would at the very least be impolite: the most likely point does seem to be before Sostratos begins his emotional speech at 381b; an exit at 381a would allow plenty of time for the costume change and would leave Getas' late arrival as a purely comic effect. The early exit for Gorgias which results is, as has been remarked, unmentioned in the text and left unmotivated: perhaps this is evidence that Menander's skill in balancing plausible motivation and the requirements of theatrical convention was not fully developed in this apparently early play.

392. *Exit* SOSTRATOS *to the left*

Sostratos has no clear exit-line, but leaves declaring his resolution and determination to take action (391–2).

393. *Enter* SIKON *from the right with a sheep*[19]

Sikon enters an empty stage and is necessarily unannounced: Sostratos must not be detained from his resolution to leave (cf. Blundell (1980) 51). The cook's arrival has however been expected since Sostratos' monologue of 260–1, and there was clearly considerable comic business accompanying the entrance, as 394–5 shows: the sheep is reluctant to move and keeps feeding on the plants on the way. Sikon is easily identified as a cook: he would carry the knife necessary for his work (cf. Handley (1965) ad loc.) and refers to himself explicitly as 'the cook' (399) with a traditional pun on κατακόπτω for which cf. GS ad loc. Handley (1970) 10–11 remarks that this entrance 'makes an immediate contrast with the mood of romantic resolution given by Sostratos' departure with his mattock for toil and hot sun' and compares the cook-scenes of *Aspis* 216ff. and *Mis.* 270ff. for similar changes of mood at the end of an act; for new developments at act-endings see on *Aspis* 246 above.

401. *Enter* GETAS *from the right with a load of baggage*

The spectacle of the overladen slave was a familiar one in Greek Comedy: its popularity in the fifth century is shown by Ar. *Ran.* 1ff.: Getas' entrance increases the comic element at the end of the act and

[19] The entrance speech has structural similarities with *Sam.* 399ff. (Nikeratos' entrance with a sheep); see T. Williams, *RhM* 105 (1962), 222–3.

prepares for the arrival of the women in the next act (434–5). The slave is identified by Sikon at 401, and if as suggested above Gorgias does leave at 381, the point of Getas' late entry will be purely comic, to emphasize the amount he is carrying which forces him to lag behind.

426. *Exeunt* GETAS *and* SIKON *to the shrine*
Sikon instructs Getas to take the luggage indoors at 419–20, and is eager to begin the preparations (420–1): he precedes Getas into the shrine, perhaps turning to go at 424 when he finishes encouraging him. Getas is less keen to begin, as 423–4 shows, probably due to the enormous load he has to carry; and he lags behind, speaking the complimentary words 425–6a to Sikon's departing back and reserving 426b as an aside until the cook has entered the cave and is out of earshot.[20]

ΧΟΡΟΥ

427. *Enter* KNEMON *from his house*
Knemon enters speaking back to the old woman within, ordering the door to be bolted, which (as GS ad loc. remark) is a sign of his misanthropy. He is leaving for work on his farm as predicted at 358–9, but his daughter is not with him (cf. 359–60).

430. *Enter* SOSTRATOS' MOTHER, PLANGON,[21] *the pipe-girl* PARTHENIS *and* MUTE SLAVES *from the right*
The group is unannounced, which contributes to the surprise effect as they burst suddenly on to the stage bringing noise and bustle: their arrival startles Knemon whose attention is directed away from the stage back into the house as he issues instructions to Simiche.

The part-distribution in 430–41 has been much discussed, mainly as to whether a speaking role should be given to Sostratos' mother and the consequences for the movements of Getas. The essential arguments are stated by GS (pp. 200–3),[22] and the solution adopted in the *OCT* is with one modification (for which see on 441 below) accepted in what follows.

[20] For further discussion, with parallels, see C(3) and on the textual difficulties of the passage see Bain (1977) 128–9.

[21] Probably Sostratos' sister; GS on 430 point out that in *Heros* and *Sam.* the name belongs to a freeborn girl.

[22] See also Goldberg (1980) 138 n. 15.

434. *Enter* GETAS *from the shrine*

Getas is unannounced and gives no explicit reason for his entrance; the audience may assume that he has heard the noise of the pipe (432) or of the group being given its orders by the mother. His arrival adds a further element of bustle to the scene, which is bound to increase Knemon's annoyance.

441. *Exeunt* SOSTRATOS' MOTHER *and* SISTER, *the* PIPE-GIRL, *and the* MUTE SLAVES *into the shrine*

The mother instructs the other members of the group to follow her inside (439): she is keen to complete the sacrifice (cf. 430–1). Arnott (1979) ad loc. may well be correct to assign 441b to Sostratos' mother, against the earlier consensus which followed H. Lloyd-Jones[23] in giving the words to Getas. Expressions similar to ποῖ κέχηνας ('what are you gaping at?') are addressed to slow-moving slaves by their masters at *Kolax* fr. 1 and *Sam.* 105[24] which suggests that it is more likely to be the mother who directs the line at a dawdling assistant, picking up the eagerness to sacrifice which was highlighted at her entrance, than for Getas to speak it either to Knemon[25] or to a fellow slave.[26]

455. *Exit* KNEMON *to his house*

Knemon leaves in considerable anger, as his monologue shows, explaining that he cannot leave his house with such a crowd next door (443–4). He has a clear exit-line (453–4), calling to the old woman to open the door, which creates a kind of ring composition with 427. His monologue both covers the off-stage time for the sacrifice (cf. GS on 442) and stresses again Knemon's general hatred of his fellow men and his particular anger at that moment before the comic scenes of attempted borrowing.

456. *Enter* GETAS *from the shrine*

Getas enters talking back to one of the party in the shrine, at once revealing his motivation: he must try to borrow a vital piece of equipment from the neighbours. Since, however, his entrance is juxta-

[23] *Dyscolus* (Oxford, 1960) ad loc.

[24] cf. Ar. *Lys.* 184, 426 and the passages collected by W. Headlam, *Herodas* (Cambridge, 1922) on iv. 42.

[25] So Lloyd-Jones (op. cit.), followed by GS 202.

[26] So J. G. Griffiths, *CR* 18 (1968), 8–11, whose attempt to establish a rule that in comedy only social equals use the form of address of a vocative adjective followed by cύ is not conclusive; see GS 202–3.

posed with Knemon's furious exit cursing the new arrivals, it is clear that the latter will not look favourably on the request. Getas' use of ἐνοχλητέον τοῖϲ γειτνιῶϲι ('we'll have to trouble the neighbours', 458) is significant since one of Knemon's more prominent words of abuse to others has been ὄχλοϲ (157, 166) and he has used the word to refer to the party in the cave (432). Getas' unfortunate use of the cognate verb here, with which compare Sikon's words at 491 before the second borrowing scene, further prepares for Knemon's violent reaction.

466. *Enter* KNEMON *from his house*

Getas moves to Knemon's door at 459, and the knocking sequence is drawn out for seven lines before the door is answered; presumably he knocks and shouts loudly, repeating παιδίον or παῖδεϲ (459, 461, 462, 463, 464) in a deliberate exploitation of the comic and slapstick associations of door-knocking in Greek Comedy.[27] The lengthy sequence increases the humour for the audience as they anticipate Knemon's enraged appearance.

The old man's furious entrance is announced by Getas with an alarmed cry ἠήν as he hears someone running to the door. As Getas' reaction shows (467) Knemon is fierce on entry: with the threat to eat him alive (468) compare Pyrrhias' prediction in act i (124).

480. *Exit* GETAS *to the shrine*

Getas makes his intention to leave plain with εὐτύχει (476), a term of farewell (cf. *Epitr.* 370) and an announcement of his intention to report back to the women (478–9). He leaves with a comically elevated invocation of the gods (479b: compare the genuine emotion of the phrase at 202, 381) and a despairing description of Knemon (480); these lines are probably delivered as an aside.[28] Of the earlier part of his speech, 475 may also be an aside (so Arnott (1979)) or may be spoken to Knemon (so GS on 476): in view of the more respectful tone of βέλτιϲτε ('sir', 476) and the fictitious explanation of the mission (476b–7), the former interpretation is probably more likely.

486. *Exit* KNEMON *to his house*

As with his previous departures (178, 455) Knemon leaves with a speech confirming his hatred of people and social life; since he is fuming with rage there is no clear exit-line.

[27] See B(5)(*a*) above.

[28] Cf. GS on 476; Bain (1977) 129.

487. *Enter* SIKON *from the shrine*

Sikon appears talking back to Getas inside the shrine, and it emerges from his speech that he too intends to approach Knemon. This scene recalls in many ways the preceding attempt of Getas to borrow a pot: both are comically juxtaposed with a furious exit of Knemon, both begin with an entry talking back, and both culminate in violent knocking and angry response.[29] These obvious structural similarities produce a notable comic effect: before knocking Sikon delivers a monologue of self-praise describing his skills in approaching different sorts of people; but, as the audience knows, he is sure to fail on this occasion.

500. *Enter* KNEMON *from his house*

Knemon bursts out in response to Sikon's knock with πάλιν αὖ cύ; ('you again, is it?', 500). Here he does not mistake Sikon for Getas, nor is the address evidence for Getas' silent presence so that he and not the cook receives the force of Knemon's anger, as some have supposed (see n. 29 above): rather, the old man's earlier reaction to strangers has been to class them as a group and not as individuals, so that at 167–8 he speaks not directly to Sostratos but fulminates generally at mankind using plural not singular verbs (173 ff.). So here Sikon simply represents another intrusion, and his actual identity is of little consequence.

At 502 Knemon calls to Simiche indoors for a strap: τὸν ἱμάντα δόc, γρᾶυ ('give me the strap, old woman'). GS on 504 doubt that the order is carried out, and almost certainly it was not. It appears not to have been uncommon during heated exchanges in comedy to call for a strap when one's opponent was reluctant to do as he was told, as the following examples illustrate;[30] at *Sam.* 321–2 Demeas calls: ἱμάντα παίδων τις δότω | ἐπὶ τουτονί μοι τὸν ἀcεβῆ ('one of you slaves, give me a strap to use on this wretch'); Moschion threatens to do the same (*Sam.* 662–3): εἰ λήψομαι | ἱμάντα ('if I get a strap'). From Middle Comedy cf. Antiphanes fr. 74 Kock 7–8 where the context shows that

[29] The similarities of the scenes tell against the proposal of Handley (1965) and Arnott (1979) that Getas may accompany Sikon here, and that the entrance is consequently in mid-conversation. The possibilities for comic business are of course limitless if Getas is imagined to be on-stage, and a possible sequence of action is set out by GS on 478–9; however, as GS remark, there is nowhere an obvious point at which Getas could subsequently leave the stage, and in addition there is nowhere an explicit reference to him; more importantly, an entrance in mid-conversation would disrupt the series of parallels between this scene of approach to Knemon and that which preceded it.

[30] See Austin (1970) ad loc. for further parallels.

the speaker does not get the strap: ἔξω τις δότω | ἱμάντα ('someone give me a strap out here').[31] Here in *Dysk.* and in the closely similar passage *Sam.* 321 the dialogue and action continue at such a pace that not only would the audience over look the non-fulfilment of the order[32] but a silent appearance by Simiche in *Dysk.* or by an unnamed mute in *Sam.* would provide an unwelcome distraction from the angry confrontation.

514. *Exit* KNEMON *to his house*
Knemon leaves with an expression of exasperation which replaces an explicit exit-line (as at 178 above).

521. *Exit* SIKON *to the shrine*
Sikon departs having rejected the idea of trying another neighbour, deciding instead to roast the meat (518–19). His exit monologue is lengthy and deliberative (cf. Blundell (1980) 53) and may be intended to lessen the contrast of the violent swift scenes which have just taken place with the appearance of Sostratos who is to deliver a long and reflective monologue.

522. *Enter* SOSTRATOS *from the left*
Sostratos' entrance marks a complete change of tone from the preceding scenes: he is exhausted, and in contrast to his first appearance when he was instantly recognizable as a rich young man, he is no longer wearing his luxurious cloak, probably having taken it off at 370–1 (see GS on 371: there is no need to suppose he deposits it in the shrine at that point, as he may simply return carrying it at 522),and is sunburn't (535, cf. 734). His first words pick up Sikon's parting speech with a reference to Phyle (522, cf. 521): this is both amusing for the audience[33] and, as Handley (1965) ad loc. remarks, serves to reintroduce Sostratos to them after his absence. His motivation for returning is kept until after his narrative monologue (cf. Blundell (1980) 53–4) and even then is vague: he is simply a lover

[31] A further fourth-century example comes in Dem. *Fals. Leg.* 197 where party guests, angered by the Olynthian girl, order ἱμάντά τις φερέτω and the scholiast comments on the representation of characters 'maddened by drink and by desire, as in a play'.

[32] In comedy orders to slaves could be disregarded without any specific reason; see Bain (1981) 44–7, and on unfulfilled threats in Greek drama cf. G. Zuntz, *Entretiens Hardt*, 6 (1960), 207.

[33] For examples of similar devices in Roman Comedy see W. G. Arnott, *BICS* 19 (1972), 60.

drawn to his beloved's house,[34] a statement which reminds the audience of Pan's declared role in the affair.

546. *Enter* GETAS *from the shrine*
Getas emerges suddenly and unannounced, bursting on to the stage talking back to Sikon and complaining about the amount of work he has to do. His arrival is dramatically necessary for his meeting with Sostratos, yet his actual motivation for appearing is not made explicit: both Handley (1965) and GS compare the entrance of Karion at Ar. *Plut.* 821: ἐμὲ δ' ἐξέπεμψεν ὁ καπνός· οὐχ οἷος τε γὰρ | ἔνδον μένειν ἦν. ('the smoke drove me outside; I couldn't stay indoors'). However, this comparison only highlights the absence of explicit motivation in Menander, where the audience can only assume that Getas comes out to escape the demanding cook and to remove the smoke from his eyes (559): see my remarks on *Epitr.* 382–3. Sostratos addresses Getas at 551 but the slave fails to recognize him due both to the blinding smoke and, probably, Sostratos' dishevelled appearance.

573. *Exit* SOSTRATOS *to the left*
Sostratos states his motivation, to fetch Gorgias and Daos, at 558–9 and leaves with a passing reference to Pan (571–2), reminding the audience that despite the apparent obstacle posed by Knemon, the proposed marriage is still subject to divine guidance. GS on 573 remark that Sostratos' parting assurance of success marks a sharp contrast with Simiche's frantic entrance.[35]

574. *Enter* SIMICHE *from* KNEMON'*s house*
Simiche enters in a frenzy just as Sostratos leaves with his optimistic prediction (571–2): her entrance in high emotion is made more surprising by being unannounced, and her first line (574) has an elevated tone, on whose comic effect see Handley (1965) ad loc. This is the second of a series of three emotional entrances from Knemon's house with news about the well (189, 574, 620) all of which make use of tragic associations of various kinds to achieve their effects, whether to underline the importance of a scene at 189 or for comic effect as here; cf. Blundell (1980) 55. The audience is accordingly prepared for the importance of the well in the plot.

[34] For entrance monologues gripping the audience's attention by the content of speech, with entrance motivation held back at the end GS on 545 compare *Perik.* 172–80; see also *Epitr.* 878–907.

[35] For further examples of exit-lines relegated for dramatic effect see C(5)(*a*) above.

588. *Enter* KNEMON *from his house*
Simiche delivers a door announcement (586) which comes at the climax of her description of Knemon's anger indoors at her loss of the mattock (584–5) and which creates a sense of panic at his imminent arrival which infects even the previously unsympathetic Getas (587–8a). Knemon bursts on to the stage in a fury looking for the old woman, as his first words make clear.[36]

596. *Exit* SIMICHE *to* KNEMON'*s house*
The old woman leaves in obedience to Knemon's orders of 596 repeated from 589–90.

601. *Exit* KNEMON *to his house*
Knemon leaves without an explicit exit-line, his intention to depart having been plain since his dismissal of Simiche and his decision to descend into the well (598). His actual parting words are a refusal of help in the form of a strong curse made emphatic by its position, and once again his exit emphasizes his antisocial character. Getas speaks an exit acknowledgement which reflects the speed of the old man's departure εἰϲ]πεπήδηκεν ('he's leapt inside', 602).[37]

611. *Enter* SOSTRATOS, GORGIAS, *and* DAOS *from the left*
Getas delivers a visual announcement at the end of this monologue (607–8).[38] Despite the lack of any explicit indication of the slave's presence in the rest of the act, it is not certain that he leaves for the shrine now (Bain (1977) 110 n. 5) as his question of 610–11—where ἄγει is surely third-person ('he is bringing') and not addressed to Sostratos (see GS ad loc.)—reveal his curiosity about the new arrivals, and he may withdraw silently to observe unseen.

Sostratos and Gorgias enter in mid-conversation, and the impression of a continuing dialogue is best conveyed by the part-divisions proposed by Webster[39] and adopted by Arnott (1979), assigning πάντ' ἔχομεν (i.e. 'no, really', 612) to Gorgias as a refusal.

[36] On the phrase used see B(4) above.

[37] For an identical acknowledgement of a furious exit cf. *Sam.* 564 and see C(5)(*b*) above.

[38] Accepting the three-actor rule, Getas' monologue serves to cover the time during which the actors playing Knemon and Simiche change and move from the *skene*-building to the side; Daos is played by a mute. The visual announcement comes four and a half lines before Sostratos speaks, and may be delivered before the actors become visible to the audience in an attempt to conceal the time needed for the costume change.

[39] *PACA* 4 (1961), 45; cf. GS ad loc.

619. *Exeunt severally:* SOSTRATOS, GORGIAS, *and* GETAS *to the shrine,* DAOS *to* GORGIAS' *house*

Gorgias accompanies Sostratos to the shrine, reluctantly accepting his invitation and sending Daos off under orders to look after his mother. GS n. 617 are probably correct to view the fuss over Daos' whereabouts as simply the removal of a character who is not needed again and whose help in rescuing Knemon is not required. Getas, if indeed he did not go off at 611, perhaps precedes Sostratos into the shrine, silent and unnoticed.

ΧΟΡΟΥ

620. *Enter* SIMICHE *from* KNEMON'*s house*

Simiche appears with the third of the three emotional entrances from Knemon's house, on which see 574 above.

621. *Enter* SIKON *from the shrine*

Sikon enters in response to Simiche's cries, angry at the disturbance (621–3). There are broad similarities with the previous entrance of the old woman (574ff.): in both scenes the emotional entrance-line is followed by an account of what has happened indoors in the presence of an (initially at least) unsympathetic listener—in the earlier scene Getas who made aside comments, here Sikon who makes facetious suggestions.

635. *Enter* GORGIAS *from the shrine*

Simiche has no reason to know that Gorgias is in the shrine rather than his house, and her cry at 635a may indeed be a sign of despair when he fails to appear at once; so GS ad loc. Arnott (1979) supposes that the old woman actually knocks on Gorgias' door as she shouts; but this is unlikely as Daos is inside and might be expected to answer the knocking, which would be an unnecessary complication. Gorgias enters in response to her summons, and it is an indication of the depth of the crisis that the slave-woman transgresses what appears to have been the usual social limits on the device and calls her social superior on to the stage.[40]

638a. *Enter* SOSTRATOS *from the shrine*

Sostratos appears in response to Gorgias' summons.

[40] See B(5)(*b*) above.

638b. *Exeunt* GORGIAS, SOSTRATOS, *and* SIMICHE *to* KNEMON'*s house*
Gorgias orders Simiche to lead the way in: that this is the meaning of the dicolon in the papyrus after δεῦϱ' ('this way') is suggested both by the probably identical punctuation at 177 to indicate change of addressee (see note on 178) and by the absence in δεῦϱ' of the *scriptio plena* normal at speaker changes. There is no implausibility in Gorgias needing guidance: he may after the lapse of many years be unfamiliar with the layout of Knemon's house; so GS ad loc.

665. *Exit* SIKON *to the shrine*
Sikon leaves without an explicit exit-line, but presumably goes to continue his duties in the shrine: the reason for his original appearance was to discover the cause of the noise, and he has now no further business on stage. There is no indication of his presence in the following scene, and the third speaking actor is needed to play Knemon at 691 ff. Sikon turns to call (660–1) to the women in the shrine as he leaves.

666. *Enter* SOSTRATOS *from* KNEMON'*s house*
Sostratos emerges unannounced on to an empty stage, beginning his monologue with an impressive oath which reflects his emotional state.[41] The audience's curiosity at events indoors has been aroused by Sikon's monologue (639–40) in which, commenting on the off-stage noises of 648–9,[42] he appears to have revealed that Knemon has not actually died (648, perhaps elaborated in the lacuna). Sostratos is however too absorbed in his feelings for the girl to concentrate on Knemon's fate and his opening sentence teases the audience by suggesting that the old man is in fact dead, an impression only dispelled by the last word μικϱοῦ ('nearly', 669; cf. GS ad loc.). Sostratos keeps back his own motivation for leaving the house until the end of the monologue (685–6), having intrigued the audience with this account of events indoors.

The juxtaposition of the two long monologues of Sikon and Sostratos is notable and, although they are comic and lively, has the effect of slowing down the action considerably; following the farcical and swift scenes of act iii—the arrival of the party, the repeated attempts to borrow a pan, Simiche's panic-stricken entrance—and the dramatic opening to act iv, the pace of the action is carefully reduced

[41] Cf. Handley (1965) ad loc.; Blundell (1980) 57–8.

[42] For a similar interpretation of off-stage noises cf. *Sam.* 364, 553 and note Aulus Gellius on *Plokion* (404K).

in preparation for the long and important speech of the stricken Knemon (702 ff.).

690. *Enter* KNEMON, GORGIAS, *and* KNEMON'*S* DAUGHTER *from his house*[43] The flow of Sostratos' monologue is interrupted as he breaks off his sentence to announce the noise of the door opening (689); entrances which involve interrupted speech convey a sense of speed and surprise,[44] and here the arresting effect of Knemon's stricken appearance is underlined by this unexpected interruption to the monologue. GS 239–41 argue that the *ekkyklema* is used here, on the grounds both of the lack of any actual motivation for his entrance, a problem which vanishes if this conventional means by which the interior could be made visible was used (cf. Handley (1965) on 690), and the enhancement of the serious effect of the following scene of recantation which would result from the clear reference to the practice of tragedy;[45] the virtually inescapable restoration of 758 (Knemon's exit-line) shows at the very least that he enters on something wheeled: εἰϲκυ]κλεῖτ' εἴϲω με ('roll me indoors'). Webster (1974) 82 suggested that instead of the *ekkyklema* proper Menander used a wheeled bed to bring Knemon on, pointing out that in fifth-century drama the *ekkyklema* was apparently used only from the central door, and doubting whether the playwright would destroy the obvious symmetry whereby Pan's shrine is flanked by the two houses[46] to give Knemon's house the central position; cf. Handley (1965) on 758. Under Webster's proposal the wheeled bed coming from the side door could still represent an allusion to the tragic *ekkyklema*, and the audience would accept it as a comic equivalent. This seems entirely plausible, and the arrangement would still bring with it the required tragic associations alluded to above. Knemon, then, probably enters on a wheeled bed, and the significance of his plight as marking the turning point of the play is stressed by allusion to the tragic *ekkyklema*, not by use of the device itself.

[43] There is no evidence that Simiche is also present in the following scene, but if so she is played by a mute and remains in the background.

[44] Cf. *Epitr.* 442; *Sam.* 440, 532.

[45] Some deny the use of any such device in fifth-century drama, but see the bibliography of GS (pp. 239–40) and cf. Taplin (1977) 442–3. On the tragic associations in *Dysk.* see Handley (1965) on 690, 692.

[46] So Lloyd-Jones's (op. cit. n. 23 above) stage direction on 1; cf. GS on 5.

700. *Exit* GORGIAS *to his house*

Gorgias leaves to fetch his mother in response to Knemon's order (698). The papyrus has a paragraphos under 698, indicating a speaker-change, but no corresponding dicola to indicate where the new speaker began and finished; for the alternatives see GS ad loc. If the paragraphos is not a mistake, ὥϲ ἔνι μάλιϲτα ('as quickly as I can') may well be a response by Gorgias to the instruction,[47] as he is eager to carry it out and see his family reconciled: this also prompts him to say 699b–700a as an aside before leaving. At this point Knemon resumes speaking and addresses his daughter (700b). This involves assuming missing dicola after μητέρα (698) and ἔοικε (700); cf. Handley (1965) on 699–700. The objections of GS to Gorgias speaking here are unconvincing: the two examples they cite of a character dispatched on an errand who does not respond verbally both involve orders by masters to slaves (*Perik.* 755; *Sik.* 395). Here there is a positive reason for Gorgias to speak; to indicate his eagerness to fetch his mother and reconcile his family.

703–8. *Enter* GORGIAS *with his mother from his house*

758. *Exeunt* KNEMON, MYRRHINE, *and the* DAUGHTER *to* KNEMON'*s house*

Knemon orders that he be wheeled back indoors, and his abrupt exit signals the finality of his decision not to be troubled over social matters, even the marriage of his own daughter. Myrrhine and the girl probably leave with him; at 855 Gorgias goes to Knemon's house to fetch them to the feast, and now is the most convenient moment for them to leave.

773. *Enter* KALLIPPIDES *from the right*

Sostratos' visual announcement of his father enables Gorgias to reveal, as he approaches and before contact is made, that he knows Kallippides already as a good and rich farmer, an independent observation which confers an individual status on the character; cf. GS on 775. His late arrival is dramatically convenient,[48] but left unexplained; cf. Handley (1965) on 775 ff. Kallippides' entrance has a comic touch as he proclaims his hunger, and this serves to slow down the pace and reduce the tension of the act before the choral interlude; cf. my note on *Aspis* 246.

[47] For further examples of acknowledged orders see C(2) above.

[48] For εἰϲ καλόν in a visual announcement cf. *Sam.* 280.

780. *Exit* KALLIPPIDES *to the shrine*
Kallippides leaves encouraged by Sostratos, with an acknowledgement confirming his eagerness.

783. *Exeunt* GORGIAS *to* KNEMON'*s house,* SOSTRATOS *to the shrine*
Sostratos leaves to talk privately with his father, encouraged by Gorgias (781–2) who announces he will wait indoors (782–3).

ΧΟΡΟΥ

784. *Enter* SOSTRATOS *and* KALLIPPIDES *from the shrine*
Sostratos and his father enter in mid-conversation, and the interest of the audience is guaranteed by the opening words which give the impression that Kallippides' objection is to his son's marriage: this at once picks up, and suggests an unexpected twist to, the course of events before the act-break, but the impression is quickly dispelled. No reason is given for the couple to leave the cave now; Handley (1965) on 784ff. suggests that they come out to look for Gorgias, but there is no evidence for this assumption and it is more likely that, as elsewhere,[49] the technique of entry in mid-conversation is used to grip the audience's attention and conceal the lack of motivation for an appearance which is dramatically necessary to tie up the ends of the plot.

821. *Enter* GORGIAS *from* KNEMON'*s house*
Kallippides finally agrees to his son's request for a double marriage and Sostratos announces that he will summon Gorgias, at which the young farmer enters declaring that he was coming out anyway and has been eavesdropping (presumably at least from 793) by the door. From the text it is not at once obvious how this scene was staged, but it is unlikely that Gorgias was seen earlier at the doorway since this would distract attention from the conversation on stage; cf. GS ad loc. Rather this entrance represents, as Handley (1965) on 821–2 comments, a dramatic short cut whereby Gorgias' timely appearance avoids a repetition before the audience of the marriage offer, and where the dramatic convenience compensates for the absence of any explicit motivation for him to leave the house: cf. GS ad loc.[50]

[49] See B(6) above.

[50] For another dramatic short cut involving a convenient entrance and improbabilities of timing cf. *Aspis* 399 and my note ad loc.

854. *Exit* GORGIAS *to* KNEMON'*s house*
Gorgias leaves to summon his mother and sister (847–8) and Knemon (852–3) to the party in the shrine.

860. *Exit* KALLIPPIDES *to the shrine*
Kallippides leaves to prepare for the wedding celebrations (858–9) and Sostratos calls after him in encouragement.[51] His departure allows Sostratos a short soliloquy (see Blundell (1980) 61) and enables the actor playing the father to change and enter at 874 as Simiche.

866. *Enter* GORGIAS *with his* MOTHER *and* SISTER *from* KNEMON'*s house*
Gorgias reappears, unannounced but expected, shepherding his no doubt surprised mother and sister. His report on Knemon serves to prepare for the final scenes of torment: while to some extent the old man had won the audience's sympathy in his speech of act iv, his continuing unsociability and rudeness is revealed here by his refusal to join the party (868–9).

867. *Exeunt* MOTHER *and* GIRL *to the shrine*
The couple are sent off by Sostratos, who speaks to his mother who probably remains inside the cave; cf. GS on 867.

873. *Exeunt* SOSTRATOS *and* GORGIAS *to the shrine*
Gorgias delays departure into the shrine as urged by Sostratos (871a) to voice his embarrassment at meeting unknown women, an example of a delayed exit for characterization.[52] The couple's exit to the celebrations completes the love-plot of the play.

874. *Enter* SIMICHE *from* KNEMON'*s house*
Knemon had earlier asked Gorgias to take Simiche with him (868), but her entrance now, apparently of her own accord (874) may have been kept separate to make possible her strong condemnation of Knemon's character before his discomfiture. Blundell (1980) 79–80 is probably correct to argue that Simiche's words are an imaginary address to Knemon rather than actually spoken back to him; he points out that it would be odd if Knemon, who is said to be asleep at 893 and certainly so when brought out at 909, were to be supposed to be awake at 874. It could be added that Simiche would hardly address such abusive comments to the master who inspired such terror in her earlier in the

[51] See C(3) above.
[52] See C(4) above.

play if there was a chance he might hear. The mode of delivery would of course make this clear in performance.

879. *Enter* GETAS *from the shrine*

Getas enters unannounced talking back to an unidentified person in the shrine who has sent him on an errand to see how Knemon is; cf. the similar entrance-line of a character with an errand at *Perik.* 181. By 893 Getas has learnt that Knemon is asleep, information not volunteered by Simiche: accordingly he may look through Knemon's door in fulfilment of his mission at some point in the lacunose 887–8; cf. GS on 886.

The pipe-player now begins to play, and Getas addresses him at 880. His actual whereabouts and identity are unclear; Lloyd-Jones[53] brings him or her on from the shrine with Getas, and it may be that it is Parthenis, the party's musician (432), who plays here. Other suggestions include Donax, the slave referred to at 959; see GS on 959. However, it may be best to imagine that the pipe-player not as a character of the play but as the musician who accompanied the choral dances in the interludes and who may be visible at the side of the stage or in the orchestra: Getas' address to him is a thorough breach of the dramatic illusion before the final scenes of torment; cf. Handley (1965) on 880.

885. *Exit* SIMICHE *to the shrine*

Simiche leaves with a clear exit-line (883–4), encouraged by Getas (884–5).

890. *Enter* SIKON *from the shrine*

Sikon enters in response to Getas' shout (888–9).

908. *Exit* SIKON *to* KNEMON'*s house*

GS ad loc. suggest that Getas and Sikon may both briefly enter the house to fetch Knemon, with the music of the pipe serving to cover the empty stage. However, an empty stage flanked by the departure and re-entrance of the same character or characters was a notable rarity in Greek drama[54] and it is equally likely that one of the conspirators remained on-stage while the other fetched Knemon. If so, which one? The problem is compounded by the complete uncertainty of the part-attributions in the papyrus from 900; see GS on 900ff., whose division

[53] Op. cit. (above, n. 23), stage direction on 879.

[54] Cf. Taplin (1977) 362.

of speeches is accepted here. If Getas is accordingly assigned all the imperatives directly to do with the plan, Sikon may carry the old man out (cf. 908–9), in which case Getas may remain by the door as he does so. At 906–7 Sikon lingers on stage before obeying Getas' instruction to go indoors, fearful that the latter will abandon him, an example of a delayed exit for characterization; cf. on 873.

909. *Enter* SIKON *with* KNEMON *from* KNEMON'*s house*
There is no way of knowing the means by which Knemon is brought on; GS on 908 record some suggestions. If as proposed above only Sikon enters to fetch him, the most likely possibilities are that he is carried out asleep in the cook's arms, or is perhaps pushed out on a wheeled bed, an appearance which would comically recall his last entrance in a similar manner where there was a clear allusion to the tragic *ekkyklema* (690 ff.).

960. *Enter* DONAX *from the shrine*
The mute slave Donax enters in response to the summons (959) to take the defeated Knemon into the shrine. Cύ γε (959) has met with little favour, and of the proposed emendations Lloyds-Jones' cύ τ' Cίκων ('and you too, Sikon') is perhaps best; the introduction of a second mute from the shrine as implied by reading the proper name Cύρε (Maas) seems unnecessary.

964a. *Enter a* MUTE SLAVE *from the shrine*
Another mute now appears in response to the order of 963 to hand out the torches and garlands traditional at the triumphant finales of comedies.[55] Arnott (1979) ad loc. cannot be correct that Donax has brought these things out, since he responds to his summons (960) before they are requested (964).

964b. *Exeunt* DONAX *and* SIKON *carrying* KNEMON, *accompanied by the* MUTES
Knemon is carried off in accordance with Getas' instructions (960) and Getas is left alone on stage to address the audience. The papyrus has a paragraphos under 984 and a dicolon after δαῖδα which suggests a change of speaker; Sikon cannot speak the final five lines to the audience as he is now carrying Knemon, as GS ad loc. point out; but if a second dicolon has been omitted after λαβέ (964b), 'take this' could

[55] Cf. W. G. Arnott, *Hermes*, 93 (1965), 253–5. On the use of mutes to bring garlands see A(2) above.

plausibly be assigned to the cook as he places a garland on the reluctant Knemon, completing his humiliation before carrying him off.

969. *Exit* GETAS *to the shrine*
Getas leaves having delivered the apparently formulaic appeal for applause and victory which is found in more or less identical form in every surviving final scene from Menandrean comedy;[56] 998–9 are repeated verbatim at *Mis.* 465–6 and *Sik.* 422–3, while *Sam.* 733–7 is a close counterpart.[57]

[56] Cf. S. Dworacki, *SPhP* 3 (1977), 35–40.

[57] Cf. further Menander frag. 771 K.-T.; Poseidippos *CGF* 218; Antiphanes *CGF* 3; *CGF* 249 (*adespoton* of New Comedy).

5

Epitrepontes

142. *Enter* HABROTONON *from* CHAIRESTRATOS' *house*

When the fragment begins, an eavesdropping scene with Smikrines and Chairestratos is in progress.[1] Habrotonon enters unannounced, and her motivation is at once clear from her direct address to Chairestratos: she has been sent to summon him indoors, and knows exactly where he will be.[2] Although the new entrant's identity is not explicit in the papyrus there are strong reasons for assuming it to be the hetaera, i.e. the use of γλυκύτατε ('my dearest', 143) which may well form part of her linguistic characterization, cf. γλυκεῖα ('my darling', 862),[3] and her remark in favour of the disruption of households (166–7) which would be best understood if spoken by an hetaera who would be likely to gain by such circumstances.

As Habrotonon is unannounced and unidentified, GS on 142ff. suggest she may have appeared already, which would also explain her apparent certainty over Chairestratos' whereabouts: but her reason for taking part in an earlier scene and the cause of her withdrawal to the house cannot now be recovered, beyond the fact that she would not have left earlier on seeing Smikrines approach, since at 143 she asks who he is.

163. *Exit* SMIKRINES *to* CHARISIOS' *house*

Smikrines may in the lacuna have observed Habrotonon and Chairestratos (so GS on 149–60) but due to the difficulties of part-division this is uncertain; cf. Bain (1977) 111. He now leaves to see his daughter, a movement presumably expected since his arrival on stage, and delivers an explicit exit-line (160–1): his parting speech reflects his anger and determination as he reveals his plans, ending with his intention to tackle Charisios, where the choice of word is significant; GS ad loc. define προcβαλῶ (163) as a military term. The effect of his exit is indicated by Chairestratos' reaction οἷον κίναδοc ('what a fox!', 165).

1 Likely reconstructions of the opening scenes are given by GS 291–4; Webster (1974) 137; Arnott (1979) 386–9.

2 Cf. the entrance of Syrus at Ter. *Ad.* 882.

3 On Habrotonon's characteristic use of endearments cf. Webster (1974) 102.

171. *Exeunt* CHAIRESTRATOS *and* HABROTONON *to* CHAIRESTRATOS' *house*

Habrotonon entered at 142 to summon Chairestratos indoors and her suggestion that they now leave is taken up (168–9). The original motivation to leave is now supplemented by two new reasons: first, the urgent need to inform Charisios of Smikrines' arrival (164–5); and secondly, the conventional announcement of, and withdrawal before, the first entry of the chorus.[4]

The entry of Habrotonon is followed by a flurry of departures just before the act-break: on the introduction of a new element towards the end of the act see my note on *Aspis* 246.

ΧΟΡΟΥ

172. *Enter* ONESIMOS *from* CHAIRESTRATOS' *house*
[*Enter Smikrines from Charisios' house*]
[*Exit Onesimos to Chairestratos' house*]

Once again the identity of the new entrant (172ff.) is unclear from the highly fragmented papyrus, but the act probably began with a slave's monologue; cf. GS on 172–7. Reconstruction of the action in the lacuna can provide further help toward identification. One certain element is the entrance of Smikrines, on stage already at 222, who may in a monologue relate his experiences in the house and describe his plan of action; as Blundell (1980) 32 points out, he says nothing on these subjects when he leaves at 371 and so has probably spoken of them earlier. A likely element in the lacuna is a meeting of the slave Onesimos and Smikrines; Webster (1960) 37 remarks that at 580–1 Onesimos withdraws before the approaching Smikrines in fear that he has discovered 'the truth', which suggests an earlier meeting in which the slave deliberately misled him (perhaps over Charisios' whereabouts; see GS on 172ff.). Such a scene perhaps fits better at the start of act ii than in the lost portions of act i before Smikrines sees his daughter. Onesimos could then be the speaker of 172–3, sent out perhaps by Charisios to spy on Smikrines and report back to him.[5] This may have been followed by Smikrines' entrance and Onesimos'

[4] Cf. on *Aspis* 249, and note that *Epitr.* 171 = *Dysk.* 232. In the passage of *Dysk.* compare the suppression of Daos' original reasons for departure and the additional motivation of the approach of the first chorus.

[5] Cf. W. E. Muir, *CR* 53 (1939), 63.

exit after a scene of dialogue, leaving the old man alone to reflect on events before the arbitration scene.[6]

218. *Enter* SYRISKOS,[7] *his* WIFE *carrying the baby, and* DAOS *from the country*
It is unclear from the papyrus whether 218 is the first line of the new scene. If it is, the entrance of the slaves hurling accusations in an angry dispute would have considerable dramatic effect, particularly if it formed a contrast with a monologue of Smikrines just before (see on 172): if a few lines of dialogue preceded 218, the slaves may still have entered in mid-conversation.[8] Daos carries a bundle with the trinkets in it (363); Syriskos' wife, a mute,[9] carries the baby (302).

How Smikrines is occupied when the new entrants arrive is not entirely clear: he may be standing in silent reflection following a monologue (so Arnott (1979) ad loc.) since his curt and irritated retort when approached (225) suggests he has been disturbed, or he may have noticed and announced the approaching slaves and then drawn back to observe them.

371. *Exit* SMIKRINES *to the city*
Syriskos asks the old man to wait to ensure Daos hands over the trinkets (364b–5) which suggests that at 364a Smikrines makes a movement to leave; he was originally reluctant to adjudicate and may have considered his presence no longer necessary when the transfer of trinkets began. The delayed exit, as often, focuses attention on a dramatically important scene, here the fate of the crucial recognition tokens.[10] When Syriskos confirms that he has everything, Smikrines resumes his exit movement (367b–9a) and at 370–1a Syriskos gratefully bids him farewell; for εὐτύχει ('farewell') in parting cf. *Dysk.* 476. Smikrines leaves to the city, whence he returns at 577: his motivation, presumably given on entry at the start of act ii, is now lost in the lacuna there.

[6] An interval with Smikrines alone on stage would be necessary under the three-actor rule to allow the actor playing Onesimos to change to play one of the rustics in the arbitration scene.

[7] On the form of the name see GS on 270; Goldberg (1980) 134 n. 11.

[8] For entrances in mid-conversation with dispute between the speakers cf. *Dysk.* 784; *Epitr.* 714; *Perik.* 467.

[9] There is dumb-show at 380: under the three-actor rule she cannot speak.

[10] See C(4) in the first part of this book.

376. *Exit* DAOS *to the country*
Daos leaves with a threat and a warning (373–5) and Syriskos retorts with an insult cast at his departing back (376a) which goes unanswered and so emphasizes his victory over his opponent.[11]

382. *Enter* ONESIMOS *from* CHAIRESTRATOS' *house*
Onesimos enters complaining in a short monologue of the cook's slowness, and Wilamowitz (1926) 70–1 remarks that his words on entry would put the audience in mind of what was probably the first scene of the play with the cook (fr. 1) and conceal his lack of motivation for entry; cf. GS ad loc. This is almost certainly correct: the slave's entrance is necessary for the choreography of the coming scene, and the lack of explicit motivation is glossed over both by his words which explain why he has the time to come out (if the audience wish, they may assume he is exasperated with the cook) and by the speed with which he is incorporated into the action on stage as he notices Syriskos and his wife at 387 and enters into dialogue at 390. Blundell (1980) 16–17 compares the action at *Perik.* 774ff. where similarly a new entrant speaks an entrance monologue unnoticed by those on stage who are occupied examining recognition tokens. Onesimos' entrance brings Charisios' situation back into prominence:[12] the ring which he recognizes becomes all-important and provides tension over the act-break as the audience anticipate the results of showing it to his master.

405. *Exit* WIFE *to* CHAIRESTRATOS' *house, with the baby*
The wife leaves under Syriskos' orders (405) in what is an attempt (as GS remark on 403) to prevent Onesimos claiming the rest of the trinkets.

416. *Exit* ONESIMOS *to* CHAIRESTRATOS' *house*
The difficulties of the scene are outlined by GS on 407–18; at 411 Syriskos is aware that he and Onesimos are heading for the same house, yet as far as it is possible to tell has not explicitly been told that this is where the slave is staying. A possible solution would be for Onesimos to make a movement at some point before 411 which would indicate to Syriskos that he is going indoors; a likely time would be 410a when Onesimos, asked to keep the ring safe or to hand it back, replies that he would rather keep it, and to underline his reply may turn and move off towards the door to cut short the discussion.

[11] See C(3) above.
[12] Cf. the appreciation of the entrance by Handley (1970) 14.

Syriskos could then go after him to deliver 410–12 as he realizes his intended point of exit. Onesimos, whose movement to depart is now clear, leaves without an explicit exit-line and 414b–16a are addressed to him as he departs by Syriskos, assuring him of his agreement.

418. *Exit* SYRISKOS *to* CHAIRESTRATOS' *house*
Syriskos has no explicit exit-line, although his movement indoors has been expected since 411, and he leaves with a short exit monologue to round off the scene; Blundell (1980) 51 compares the technique at *Aspis* 94–6, 388–90; *Sam.* 614. Since the notion of a slave practising oratory and litigation would provide a comic element, his parting words (416b–18) form a light ending to an act of great dramatic importance.

ΧΟΡΟΥ

419. *Enter* ONESIMOS *from* CHAIRESTRATOS' *house*[13]
Onesimos' first words pick up the theme which featured so prominently at the end of act ii, τὸν δακτύλιον ('the ring'), and the slave goes on to recount his failure to approach his master. The content of his monologue, which at once latches on to the topic uppermost in the spectators' minds, diverts attention from the lack of explicit motivation for his entrance, although it may be assumed that he comes out to avoid Charisios and to deliberate alone.

430. *Enter* HABROTONON *from* CHAIRESTRATOS' *house*
Habrotonon enters speaking back, presumably to guests at the party who were pestering her: while her motivation is not made explicit, her words imply that she comes out to avoid their unwanted attention; cf.

[13] GS 325–6 are unconvincing in their proposal for the passage of a night during the choral interlude, and the following points may be added to the objections of W. G. Arnott, *ZPE* 24 (1977), 17–18. First, Onesimos declares that he has received the ring ἀρτίως (436) which indicates a time more recent than the previous day; so M. Cannata Fera, *GIF* 6 (1975), 134. Secondly, the entrance of Habrotonon (430) shows that the company inside has become riotous, and on arrival Smikrines assumes the meal in progresss to be an ἄριστον (609–10); accepting the passage of a night, this must mean that the party has lasted since the previous evening and up to the following lunch-time (cf. J. C. B. Lowe, *Hermes*, 111 (1983), 443 n. 76 who compares *Dysk.* 855–7), but if this is so Menander has left it puzzlingly inexplicit. Alternatively and more simply the ἄριστον of act iii is, as Arnott (op. cit.) suggests, the meal which is still awaited in act ii (cf. 382ff.); i.e. act iii is later on the same day. The illogicalities in the actions of Onesimos and Syriskos on which GS (p. 325) comment are, while perplexing, insufficient to outweigh this evidence.

Sam. 713, where Nikeratos' entrance talking back implies that he comes out to escape his wife's nagging. She fails to see Onesimos as her attention on entry is directed away from the stage back into the house: she then speaks a monologue as Onesimos, too engrossed in his thoughts to notice her, continues with his. The resulting scene provides two independent views of Charisios; cf. Blundell (1980) 29.

440–4. HABROTONON [*to herself, unaware she is not alone*]. For this is the third day I've been sitting, as they say, celibate!

ONESIMOS [*to himself, also unaware he is not alone*]. How then, by the gods, How, I beseech you . . .

SYRISKOS [*bursting out of Chairestratos' house*]. Where is he, the one I've searched the house looking for? [HABROTONON, *disturbed by the noise, turns and sees the two men and, unobserved by them, watches their encounter. Syriskos sees Onesimos.*] You there, my good fellow, give back the ring!

Syriskos enters in search of Onesimos, as his brief entrance monologue with ποῦ' cτ[ί ('where is he?') makes clear.[14] His arrival is abrupt and aggressive, interrupting Onesimos' monologue,[15] and he addresses the slave directly with οὗτοc ('You there', 443), shattering the slightly dreamy atmosphere of the opening scene. This provides the most obvious point at which Habrotonon may be roused from her state of unawareness: the text is inexplicit over the point at which this occurs, as the hetaera only subsequently indicates that she has been listening (471–2) and indeed need only have heard 451–2, when the Tauropolia is mentioned. However, if she has stayed close to Chairestratos' door, Syriskos' sudden entrance and loud address to Onesimos would naturally draw her attention, and this could be signalled to the audience by a gesture, allowing the confrontation to proceed observed; cf. Bain (1977) 139.

463. *Exit* SYRISKOS *to the city*

Syriskos leaves with an explicit exit-line (462–3), and while his departure was prepared at 445, his motivation is left unclear. Whether he returned from the city in a now lost scene is unknown: Wilamowitz (1926) 76 took ἥξω ('I shall return', 462) as evidence that he did. If so, the reason for his trip may have been explained then.

On Syriskos' departure Habrotonon approaches Onesimos who

[14] See B(4) above.

[15] For examples of entrances with interrupted speech see on *Dysk.* 690.

also expresses no surprise either at seeing her or at the obvious fact of her eavesdropping. This does not imply that he has seen her before 464 (Bain (1977) 139 n. 1 points out that οὖν ('so') rules out 441–2 as an address to her); as his short replies suggest (446–7, 470, 472–3), he is too concerned over his own plight to bother himself over Habrotonon's presence.

556. *Exit* HABROTONON *to* CHAIRESTRATOS' *house*
Habrotonon's exit has been expected since the formulation of the plan (513–14) and the handing over of the ring signals her departure (554–5). She leaves with an invocation of Πειθώ as a goddess of love and of rhetorical persuasiveness; the line emphasis the importance of the affair for the hetaera personally (so GS ad loc.) and it is thrown into prominence both by the elevated style and by its position as her parting words in place of an explicit exit-line.[16] Onesimos' comments when she has left further underline the impression of Habrotonon as a clever and resourceful woman.

582. *Exit* ONESIMOS *to* CHAIRESTRATOS' *house*
Onesimos on seeing Smikrines approaching presumably leaves to Chairestratos' house, from which he enters at 878, although additional movements in the intervening lacunae are of course possible. His wish to avoid the old man may be due to his fear that Smikrines has discovered that something the slave told him earlier was a lie (see on 172): the lengthy visual announcement increases the audience's interest and allows Onesimos time to decide to withdraw (580); Blundell (1980) 45 lists some comparable passages.[17]

583. *Enter* SMIKRINES *from the city*
Smikrines enters with a monologue so lacunose that its contents are impossible to reconstruct despite some clues, on which see GS on 583–602. There is no support in the fragmentary remains for the

[16] On this technique see C(5) above.

[17] 576 in the papyrus is unmetrical, with one excess syllable: δίδωμ' ἐμαυτοῦ τὸυϲ ὀδόνταϲ· ἀλλ' οὑτοϲί. Deleting ἀλλά to restore the metre appears the simplest course as the word is frequently added to avoid asyndeton (cf. J. Jackson, *Marginalia Scaenica* (Oxford, 1955), 103, who believed ἀλλά to have been inserted here) and a scribe with a partial familiarity with the not uncommon ἀλλά . . . γάϱ with a deictic pronoun found in Menander's visual announcements (see B(1) above) may well be responsible. However, since all other cases of visual announcements do avoid asyndeton (*DE* 30 (?); *Dyks.* 47, 607; *Sam.* 280, 639) it may be that the corruption here lies not in ἀλλά but elsewhere in the line; GS ad loc. record some suggestions.

suggestion of Webster (1974) 138 that Smikrines may have met Syriskos and heard the story of the ring from him.

[603. *Enter* KARION *and* SIMIAS *from* CHAIRESTRATOS' *house*]
[631a. *Exeunt* KARION *and* SIMIAS *to the city*]
[631b. *Enter* CHAIRESTRATOS *from his house*]
[*Exit* CHAIRESTRATOS *to the city*]
[*Exit* SMIKRINES *to* CHARISIOS' *house*]
The presence of the cook Karion as a speaker in the fragmentary scenes after 609 is indicated by the marginal Καϱ (622) but the moment of his entrance, whether 603, or 609 where he would perhaps begin an entrance monologue with ἐγώ, is uncertain; cf. GS on 603–36. He is accompanied by an attendant Simias (630) who, if the couple leave immediately before Chairestratos arrives (at 631?) is mute since the third speaking actor is required to play this new entrant.[18] The scene with Karion, Simias, and Smikrines can only broadly be reconstructed: from Smikrines' comments (609b–10a) and the cook's lament (610b–11) it appears that Karion has left the house since the party has been disrupted by Habrotonon's revelations over the ring and her claim to be the violated girl (621). Karion's words at 610–11 show no awareness of Smikrines' preceding comment (609) which suggests that the old man is eavesdropping rather than participating in the dialogue at this point (so Arnott (1979) ad loc.). At 631 Karion apparently instructs Simias to leave with him and they may now go, although there is no certainty that Karion does not speak 631–6; cf. GS on 603–36. In the following scenes very little is certain; there is no sign of the cook's presence after 636, and he and Simias may be assumed to have left, presumably back to the city. Marginal notes show that Smikrines is still on stage at 637, and Chairestratos by 690: the latter's point of entry is unclear, but he may deliver 631 ff. as an entrance monologue in amazement at events inside (so Arnott (1979) ad loc.); he and Smikrines eventually converse. Smikrines seems to address Chairestratos with a reference to Charisios (643, cf. 645), and seems to attack his son-in-law's apparent debauchery (680–1, 691–2). At the end of the scene Smikrines enters Charisios' house (from which he emerges at the start of act iv) to persuade his daughter to come home with him (655–6; cf. 714 ff.). Chairestratos' movements are less clear: he next appears on-stage at 979 ff., but whether he leaves now to his

[18] Cf. T. B. L. Webster, *CR* 15 (1965), 18; GS on 603–36.

house or to the city (which is perhaps more likely as he takes no part in the events of the next act) is uncertain.

ΧΟΡΟΥ

714. *Enter* PAMPHILE *and* SMIKRINES *from* CHARISIOS' *house*
Pamphile and Smikrines enter in mid-conversation, arguing over the old man's plan to remove his daughter from her husband's house. In the extant remains no explicit reason is given for their entrance to hold a conversation which should naturalistically have occurred inside the house; however, the characters must enter to allow the audience to witness their argument, and the couple's dramatic entrance in the midst of their dispute[19] helps the audience to overlook the lack of realistic motivation. If the first preserved line (714) is in fact the opening line of the scene (cf. Gorler (1963) 77–8) the effect of plunging into the middle of the argument with ἀλλά ('but') is particularly vivid; cf. *Geo.* 22. However, it is possible that some opening lines have been lost in which some motive for coming out may have been given.

[*Exit* SMIKRINES *to the city*]
At some point in the lacuna Smikrines, having failed to persuade his daughter, leaves to the city to fetch the nurse Sophrone (cf. 1062), probably stating his intention explicitly. On his departure Pamphile may have delivered a brief soliloquy in which fr. 8 may have featured; see GS ad loc.

Onesimos reveals later (883–4) that Charisios overheard part of the argument of Pamphile and Smikrines by listening πρὸϲ ταῖϲ θύραιϲ ('at the door'; cf. *Dysk.* 821) and Webster (1974) 138 suggests that he appears at the door and comments on the scene unnoticed by the others. This is unlikely since Onesimos' detailed account of Charisios' reaction to the conversation, even quoting his words verbatim (888 ff.), would then be an unnecessary repetition; ἀπῆλθ' εἴϲω ('he withdrew inside', 892) probably signifies withdrawal into another room inside the house rather than a movement from the stage into the house.[20]

[19] Cf. GS on 714ff.

[20] New fragments of Smikrines' conversation with Pamphile are published at *POxy.* 3532–3. They contain no evidence for the movements of the characters, and there is no reason to accept Turner's suggestion ad loc. that 3533.17/15 οἰ]κία[ν] παριϲταμένη[is spoken by Charisios from an eavesdropping position.

[*Enter* HABROTONON *from* CHAIRESTRATOS' *house, carrying the baby*]
After the lacuna the papyrus resumes with Habrotonon saying ἔξειμ' ἔχουcα ('I'll go out with [the baby]', 853). Most probably this is part at least of a sentence spoken back into the house as she enters, perhaps addressed to slaves of the household: her motivation may have been made more explicit in the preceding lacuna, but from what survives it is implied that she comes out to give the child some fresh air to stop it crying; cf. Bain (1977) 197 nn. 2, 3. GS on 853 propose as an alternative that the hetaera has been on-stage for some time already and that 853a is an announcement of her intention, having noticed Pamphile's presence and recognized her, to go in, fetch the child, and come out again, which she does while Pamphile speaks 855. However, it is fatal to this proposal that Habrotonon only becomes sure of Pamphile's identity at 860.

877. *Exeunt* PAMPHILE *and* HABROTONON, *with the baby, to* CHARISIOS' *house*
Habrotonon and Pamphile speak independently, in unawareness of each other's presence (855 ff.) and there is considerable irony as the hetaera, in a likely restoration (856), wonders when the child will find its mother. Pamphile declares she will go inside (857) and her movement to leave attracts Habrotonon's attention, causing her to call out μικρόν . . . προcμεινον ('wait a moment'; cf. 364–5); the resulting delayed exit is used to introduce a scene of considerable dramatic importance: the recognition of Pamphile as the violated girl and mother of the baby.

Habrotonon announces the noise of a door opening, heralding a new arrival, and instructs Pamphile to take her into Charisios' house so that she can learn the whole story (877). The exit avoids a repetition before the audience of facts already known to them, and Habrotonon's capable and practical character is underlined by the way she takes charge of the situation and ushers Pamphile, her social superior, off-stage.[21]

878. *Enter* ONESIMOS *from* CHAIRESTRATOS' *house*
Habrotonon delivers a door-noise announcement (874) and Onesimos now bursts on to the stage with an account of Charisios' conduct in which he repeats μαίνεται ('he's mad') four times in various forms (878–9), unable through terror to find another word (see GS ad loc.);

[21] See further C(2) n. 90 above.

his panic-stricken entrance stands in marked contrast to the optimistic departure of the women. The slave's monologue describing events within is vivid and dramatic (cf. Blundell (1980) 32–4) and his motivation for coming out—to escape possible death at Charisios' hands[22]—is reserved until the end.

908. *Enter* CHARISIOS *from* CHAIRESTRATOS' *house*
Onesimos heralds his master's appearance, probably his first in the play (cf. GS on 908), with a door announcement which focuses the audience's attention on the new entrant (906). Charisios rushes on to launch into an impassioned speech: Onesimos' monologue has prepared for his master's entrance, providing the details of his eavesdropping at the door and reaction to what he had heard, and this enables Charisios to launch directly into his self-reproach without an explanatory narrative to impede him. The tension before Charisios' appearance is deliberately increased by the elevated tone of Onesimos' language in the latter part of his monologue (cf. GS on 891), and his master's actual appearance comes as the slave at the height of anxiety is uncertain how to avoid a terrible fate (905–6). No explicit motivation is given for Charisios' entrance: he is not chasing Onesimos, and there is no evidence for the suggestion of GS on 908 that he is on his way to see Pamphile. Rather the pace of action is so swift, and the content so gripping, that the lack of motivation would go unnoticed in the audience's eagerness to see the young husband.

Onesimos' whereabouts and movements from 907 have been much debated, but the most convincing account remains that of Bain (1977) 145–7, who argues that he remains on stage during Charisios' monologue, and that his master only becomes unaware of his presence at 932b when he makes a fearful aside.[23] As a result, Onesimos' claim not to have been listening when challenged (935–6) is a lie in an attempt to save his skin.

[*Enter* HABROTONON *from* CHARISIOS' *house*]
The movements of the hetaera are obscured by the state of the papyrus. At 942 Charisios' τίϲ εἶ ϲ[ύ ('who are you?') is a surprised reaction on becoming aware of Habrotonon's presence,[24] and the

[22] For the technique of narrative preceding entry motivation see on *Dysk.* 522.

[23] 932a is part of Charisios' imagined address to Smikrines; see GS on 932; Bain (1977) 145 n. 1.

[24] The phrase does not of course mean that she is a stranger to him, but is simply an indication of surprise; Bain (1977) 146 compares *Perik.* 827; *Incerti Auctoris Fabula* (b) 10.

previous line presumably contains her first words of the scene, but when and in what circumstances she enters is wholly uncertain. The evidence of 932–4 is inconclusive: Onesimos invokes help from someone or something whose identity is lost in the gap at the end of 933; one possible solution is Wilamowitz's [γύναι ('woman'), taken as an invocation of Habrotonon which does not imply her actual presence.[25] If then 941–2 constitutes the first indication that the hetaera is on-stage, her actual entrance presumably comes shortly before these lines since it is unlikely that she could have been present for any considerable length of time beforehand without being noticed by Charisios.[26] If however Onesimos does not go to fetch her, why does Habrotonon come out now? The fragments provide no explicit clue, but the confrontation of Charisios and his slave appears to have been acrimonious and she may enter to investigate the noise in front of the house (cf. *Fab. Inc.* 20). How 941 is to be supplemented and explained remains a mystery under any of the proposed stage movements.

[*Exeunt* CHARISIOS, HABROTONON, *and* ONESIMOS *to* CHARISIOS' *house*]
Presumably Charisios leaves to be reconciled indoors with his wife: the fragments up to 958 indicate that he is at last learning the truth.

[ΧΟΡΟΥ]

[*Enter* CHAIRESTRATOS *from the city*]
These puzzling fragments and the interpretations which have been proposed are discussed by GS 369–73; the most convincing explanation yet put forward is that Chairestratos enters and delivers a monologue with self-apostrophe.[27] In it he reveals that he has a

Note however that the restoration is not certain; cf. E. G. Turner, *Themes in Drama*, ii (1980), 19.

[25] Arnott (1979) reads τουτο.γυ and prints τοῦτ' ὦ γύ[ναι, supposing Onesimos to address Habrotonon as they come on from Charisios' house; so also Turner, op. cit. 17–21. Other suggestions for the gap include [τύχη, proposed by P. G. McC. Brown, which is favoured by J. C. B. Lowe, *CR* 31 (1981), 9; however, the traces in the papyrus continue to defy interpretation (see P. G. McC. Brown, *CR* 33 (1983), 182–3).

[26] Those who bring Habrotonon on at 932 with Onesimos, supposing the slave to address her directly with [γύναι (933) have to assume that he delivers 932–4 back through the door to her before she becomes visible, or that she hangs back until 941 so that Charisios does not see her: cf. GS on 932; Arnott (1979) ad loc.

[27] Cf. T. B. L. Webster, *CR* (1965), 17; GS, p. 373; Arnott (1979) 502–3; Blundell (1980) 67–8.

passion for Habrotonon but still believes her to be the mother of Charisios' child, and so resolves to suppress his feelings: he has taken no part in the revelations of act iv and may have been in the city; see above on 631–2.

[*Enter* ONESIMOS *from* CHARISIOS' *house*]
The evidence for the slave's presence in the scene rests on the marginal speaker-identification at 1021 preserved on fragment U, which is by no means certainly to be located either at this point in *Epitr.* or indeed in this play at all; see GS 370–1. If it is to be located here, the slave's role would presumably be to inform Chairestratos of the events of the last act.

[*Enter* CHARISIOS *from his house*]
Charisios is a plausible speaker for 1060–1, apparently the concluding words of a monologue: τοιαυτηcί ('a girl such as her') refers most probably to Habrotonon (so GS ad loc.) and the speaker claims he will not touch her,but that another would not have shown such restraint, which would fit a monologue of Charisios referring to Chairestratos, perhaps spoken after the latter had left to go indoors to pursue his passion for Habrotonon; cf. Arnott (1979) 508–9.

[*Exeunt* CHAIRESTRATOS, CHARISIOS, *and* ONESIMOS *to Charisios' house*]

1062. *Enter* SMIKRINES *and* SOPHRONE *from the city*
The couple enter unannounced on to an empty stage: Smikrines had probably prepared for his return when leaving to the city in act iii; cf. GS on 1062. Sophrone is at once identified for the audience's benefit as Smikrines enters haranguing her, his first words giving the impression of a continuing conversation in which 1062ff. represents the old man's reaction to a criticism supposed to have been made by the nurse just before entry (cf. Gorler (1963) 77); for νουθετήcειc . . . με; ('are you going to give me advice?') as an indignant response to unwelcome advice compare *Sam.* 677. This technique of entry in mid-conversation is used here not merely in its usual function of a regular means by which to bring two characters on to the stage simultaneously but serves to conceal the fact that the character of Sophrone is played by a mute.[28]

[28] F. H. Sandbach, *PCPhS* 13 (1967), 44–6, has eliminated the nurse as a speaker at 1120–1. For further examples of similar concealment of mute status see B(6) above.

1078. *Enter* ONESIMOS *from* CHARISIOS' *house*

Whereas at 163 the door to Charisios' house was unlocked and Smikrines entered without knocking, he now has to summon Onesimos to open it (1075–6): this enables the following encounter to take place in front of the audience, and the resulting slight illogicality by which the door is now found to be locked would go unnoticed as the confrontation with Smikrines rapidly gets under way; so GS ad loc. Smikrines' urgency and anger are reflected in the choice and form of verb used, ἡ θύρα παιητέα ('I must hammer at the door').[29] Onesimos opens the door with a conventional response (1068a);[30] on seeing Smikrines he deliberately addresses him in the third person to annoy him.[31] The door sequence begins the farcical discomfiture of the old man.

[*Enter?*]

The two speaking actors in this scene, Smikrines and Onesimos, are both used to conceal the fact that Sophrone is played by a mute, first by the technique of entry at 1062ff. and secondly by the action at 1119–20 where the old woman indicates assent by dumb show (see n. 28 above). It appears that the third speaking actor is being kept deliberately in reserve: compare the role of the mute Pylades in Eur. *Or.* 1591–2 who is also addressed yet has no verbal response since the third speaking actor is needed to enter subsequently as Apollo.[32] GS on 1120ff. may well be right to suggest an appearance by Charisios in the now lost ending.

[29] On this point see B(5) n. 66 above.

[30] See my comments on *Aspis* 499.

[31] On this technique cf. Bain (1977) 72 n. 3; Blundell (1980) 52 n. 22.

[32] On the role of Pylades see R. P. Winnington-Ingram, *Arethusa*, 2 (1969), 130; Mastronarde (1979) 93–4.

6
Kitharistes

52. *Exeunt* A *and* B *to agora: exit slave to* B's *house*
At the suggestion of B (49–51) the two speakers leave to the agora as B promises to confide in A, and orders that some objects (ταῦτα, 51) be taken indoors; GS on 40 suggest that the reference there and in 52 is to the baggage B is supposed to have brought with him from his travels, in which case the order would be addressed to mute attendants following him on his return home. However, the circumstances may be entirely different, and it is worth noting that orders to baggage-carriers are elsewhere couched in the plural,[1] while third-person imperatives with τιϲ as here imply rather that a mute stage-hand comes forward, or out of the house, to fetch and carry.[2] This makes it unlikely that ταῦτα refers to luggage accompanying B on his return home, and suggests that he is in this scene not accompanied by a retinue of porters. However, it provides no clue to what the objects may be, nor to B's circumstances in this scene.

53. *Enter* 'G' (*Moschion's father*) *from the country*
'G' enters unannounced on to an empty stage from the country (54): his monologue explicitly conveys his motivation (54–5) and his first word καί suggests that he has entered in mid-thought; cf. Blundell (1980) 46.

65. *Exit* 'G' *to his house*
'G' leaves in search of his son, having made his intention explicit (63). An actual exit is more probable than an exit movement which is interrupted by Moschion's arrival (cf. GS on 66), as the son shows no awareness that the father for whom he is searching is present for at least three and a half lines (66–9b) before the text becomes fragmentary; indeed, the first explicit signs of meeting occur at 73–4.

66. *Enter* MOSCHION *from the city*
Moschion enters without explicit announcement as his father leaves, but G's preceding monologue serves as an implicit announcement by

[1] *Aspis* 91–2; *Dysk.* 439; *Sam.* 104–5.
[2] See A(2) in the first part of this book.

recounting how his son has summoned him to the city. Moschion is looking for his father (66–7) and probably enters from the city (so GS on 66): he cannot come from the country as it is from there that he has summoned his father, nor can he enter from G's house as he would at once meet his father in the doorway.[3] Of the remaining directions, B's house and the city, the latter is more likely, particularly in view of G's comment at 63–5. Moschion and his father each use a verbal adjective to describe their movements in search of the other (63, 66), which may reflect the urgency involved; cf. *Perik.* 266 and note ad loc.

[73. *Re-enter* 'G' *from his house*]
In the fragmentary lines G emerges, presumably on the way to the agora having failed to find Moschion inside (cf. 63–4), and greets his son with χαῖρε. At 71 Moschion may have concluded his entrance monologue with a decision to stay at home until his father arrives.

[3] Contrast Webster (1974) 157.

7
Misoumenos

A1. THRASONIDES *is discovered on stage*

The mood of the speaker is conveyed through instantly recognizable features of the opening monologue: the serious tone of the invocation of Night[1] is reinforced by the strictness of the metre (cf. GS on A1–A16), while the cause is specified as love from the first line, and the conventional claim is made to exceed all others in wretchedness (A4–A5, where GS collect parallels). The staging however is not at once explicit from the text, and while GS 438 assume that Thrasonides comes out of the house at the start of the play, the impression conveyed by the opening monologue is rather of prolonged exposure to the night: ἕcτηκ' ἐγώ ('I've taken up my position', A6) suggests that the play opens to discover Thrasonides already on stage by his door, and the reason for his presence is explained in A7. Such an opening would constitute an initial tableau such as is found in almost a quarter of surviving fifth-century tragedy, a device used when the first scene presents characters imagined to have been in certain positions on stage for some time already (for example, as suppliants in Euripides' *Andromache* and *Helen*, or struck down with illness as in *Orestes*): the first entrance of the actors to assume their places was apparently disregarded as a matter of convention.[2] *Misoumenos* is the only probable example of the device in the extant Menander (although see *Geo.* 21); but it has been argued, largely on the evidence of mosaic representations, that *Synaristosai*, the original of Plautus' *Cistellaria*, opened with an initial tableau.[3]

A15. *Enter* GETAS *from the side*

Getas' entrance provides an alternative and comic view of his master's behaviour: he enters with a monologue whose opening lines containing a down-to-earth proverb and an oath (A15–A16) contrast strongly

[1] For a general survey of such invocations see D. Del Corno, *GB* 9 (1980), 72–7.

[2] See the discussion of Taplin (1977) 134–5; P. Burian, 'The Play before the Prologue: Initial Tableaux on the Greek Stage', in J. H. D'Arms and J. W. Eadie (edd.), *Ancient and Modern: Essays in honour of G. F. Else* (Ann Arbor, 1977), 77–94.

[3] Evidence discussed and assessed by various scholars at *Entretiens Hardt*, 16 (1970), 35–9; GS, p. 12 n. 2; Newiger (1979) 487–8.

with the elevated tone of his master's speech, and he proceeds to dismiss Thrasonides' anguish as φιλοϲ[οφῶν ('he's spouting a lot of nonsense', A17). The lacunose state of A18ff. leaves a number of points unclear, not least the direction of the slave's appearance; Turner[4] remarks that it is impossible to tell from the text whether Getas enters from Thrasonides' house or from the side. However, at least the first four lines of Getas' monologue are clearly not addressed to his master nor intended for him to hear; and since Thrasonides is standing in front of his door, it is unlikely that the slave enters from the house since virtually immediate contact would be unavoidable. An entrance from the side in pursuit of his master who is walking up and down the street (A7) and who has now stopped in front of his door would explain how the slave knew precisely what Thrasonides is doing (A17, cf. A7), although exactly why he is following him is unclear from the surviving text. Getas, then, enters grumbling in a brief monologue before accosting Thrasonides; cf. Blundell (1980) 11 on the technique. The point at which contact is made on-stage between the two is simply unclear from what remains: Turner[5] cannot decide between A20 and A23, and the lack of context obscures the point of the references to the door (A20), someone having come out (A23), and the orders of the sleepers (A26).

Only a few fragments are now preserved until the third act, but the complexities of the plot and its background which can be deduced from the surviving portions of the play would almost certainly have been explained by a divine prologue[6] in act i to which GS 444 tentatively assign fr. 5; the departure of Getas and Thrasonides to clear the stage may have involved the slave's successful persuasion of his master to accompany him indoors (fr. 4?). What took place after the prologue is uncertain, but P. G. McC. Brown[7] has suggested that papyrus O19 fr. C contains the first announcement of the chorus (as was apparently conventional at the end of the first act).

175. *Exit* GETAS *to* THRASONIDES' *house*
Having made his motivation explicit (to spy on events indoors), the slave goes into his master's house from which he re-enters at 216.

[4] *POxy.* 48 (1981), 13.
[5] Ibid. 14.
[6] Cf. J. M. Jacques, 'Le Début du Misouménos et les prologues de Ménandre' in U. Reinhardt and K. Sallmann (edd.), *Musa Iocosa* (Hildesheim and New York, 1974), 77ff.
[7] *CR* 30 (1980), 6.

176. *Enter* OLD WOMAN *from* KLEINIAS' *house*
The new entrant is certainly a woman, as the female oath (176) shows; a note in the papyrus at 184 may read Γ[P]AY[C] ('OLD WOMAN'), although GS on 176 have reservations. The woman delivers a monologue reporting Demeas' behaviour whose opening sentence contains a comparison of the type found in the entrance monologues at *Dysk.* 666–7 and *Perik.* 532; cf. Blundell (1980) 58–9.

[*Enter* DEMEAS *from* KLEINIAS' *house*]
The papyrus at 185 contains the note Δ[H]MEAC, and in the previous line a speaker-change is indicated by a dicolon; the final words of the line are apparently assigned to the old woman by a marginal note (see above) and the dialogue then begins at some point in the lacunose 179–84. Presumably Demeas emerges following the old woman with questions about the swords in the house (cf. 178–9).

206. *Exit* OLD WOMAN, *presumably to* KLEINIAS' *house*
From 208 two speaking actors, Demeas and Krateia, are on-stage, and at 216 they are joined by another speaker Getas; in accordance with the three-actor rule the old woman must leave before Getas' arrival. A paragraphos under 206 suggests that her conversation with Demeas is still in progress up to that point; and she may leave with some remark at the start of that line, since there is no evidence for her presence or departure at any point during the better-preserved 208–16.

208. *Enter* KRATEIA *and* NURSE *from* THRASONIDES' *house*
Applying the three-actor rule, the nurse must be played by a mute to allow speaking parts for Krateia, Demeas, and Getas (from 216): her mute status is concealed by the entrance apparently in mid-conversation as Krateia seems to explain her motivation for entry (208; cf. GS ad loc.) which is now lost in the lacuna.[8] Her unawareness of Demeas until informed—presumably by dumb show (211; cf. GS on 202) by her nurse, who has perhaps heard 210–11 (cf. Bain (1977) 112)—shows that her entrance is unconnected with Demeas' act of knocking (206), towards which he had been working since 188 (his fruitless order to the old woman to knock); that scene was, according to Turner,[9] deliberately drawn out to heighten the tension before the reunion. The reason for Demeas' withdrawal (206–7) is explained by

[8] For further examples of entries in mid-conversation used to similar effect see B(6) above.
[9] *BICS* Suppl. 17 (1965), 12.

GS on 206, who point out that he must move back from the house to prevent a crowded scene in the doorway: another and perhaps greater benefit of withdrawal is that contact between Demeas and Krateia is postponed, allowing Krateia to explain her inability to endure something (208–9), and enabling Demeas to make an aside (210–11) which sets the elevated emotional tone for the reunion; see GS on 210–15. However, against these positive dramatic gains must be placed the resulting illogicalities of the action: Demeas knocks but moves away when he hears the door being opened,[10] and Krateia enters unaware that there has been a knock at the door just prior to her appearance. The scene requires that Demeas' attention should be firmly fixed on the door by which his lost daughter enters, and that there should be a delay before contact is made: the same effect is achieved more neatly, and without illogicalities, at *Aspis* 164 where Smikrines is prevented from actually knocking at Kleostratos' door by Daos' self-motivated appearance.

215. *Enter* GETAS *from* THRASONIDES' *house*

Getas' first words show that he is following Krateia on to the stage, presumably having been spying on her since leaving at 175 (cf. 173–4). ἐξῆλθεν ἔξω ('she came outside') is likely to be a brief entrance monologue comparable to those found with ποῦ ἐcτί[11] in such circumstances; see Blundell (1980) 12. Getas at once notices Demeas and Krateia embracing and exclaims παῖ, τί τοῦτο; ('good gracious, what's this?'): GS ad loc. aptly compare *Sam.* 691 and 715, both passages where a new entrant notices with surprise an unexpected situation on stage.

238. *Exit* GETAS *to the city*

Getas leaves at a run with explicit motivation to fetch Thrasonides, and Demeas calls after him to speed him on his way; compare *Dysk.* 860.[12]

258. *Exeunt* DEMEAS, KRATEIA, *and the* NURSE *to* THRASONIDES' *house*

Getas' report in act iv of events indoors confirms that the group leaves to Thrasonides' house, and GS on 256 suggest that Demeas will wish to meet the soldier to ransom his daughter. Whether this motivation

[10] H. Petersmann, *WS* 5 (1971), 98 n. 19, unconvincingly suggests that Demeas realizes the new entrant cannot be responding to his knocking since the door starts to open while he calls παῖ παῖδεc.

[11] See B(4) in the first part of this book.

[12] See C(3) above.

was made explicit is uncertain due to the lacunose state of the text from 250, but there is reference to something which 'must be considered' (256); Webster's ε[ἰςίωμεν ('let's go inside', 254) is perhaps unlikely in view of the exact repetition which would result in 264. The gloomy mood of the exit—whatever the precise details of the conversation, the characters appear to believe that Thrasonides has killed Krateia's brother (see GS on 246–50)—is set by 258, which probably replaces an explicit exit-line: GS ad loc. are almost certainly right to follow the papyrus O10 and to take 258 as Demeas' parting line, overruling O3 which has it as Thrasonides' entrance-line. Besides the unmistakably parallel exit-lines with ὤ at *Dysk.* 178, 514 and *Perik.* 360, such an attribution much better suits Thrasonides' mood on entry, balanced between his hopes of happiness and despair (260–1): 258 is, on the other hand, clearly spoken by a character stricken with grief.

259. *Enter* THRASONIDES *and* GETAS *from the city*

The couple enter in mid-conversation as Thrasonides with an apistetic question φήις; ('so you say . . .?')[13] summarizes the account Getas is supposed to have given him just prior to entry. This both reminds the audience of the motivation for the entrance (Getas' mission to fetch his master, 238) and conceals the fact that since two speaking actors have just left (258) and Thrasonides is played by the third, Getas must here be mute;[14] compare my comments on 208 above. The contrast between Demeas' sorrowful departure viewing Thrasonides as his son's murderer, and the soldier's excited entrance (cf. 266) unaware of what he is supposed to have done creates considerable irony.

269. *Exeunt* THRASONIDES *and* GETAS *to* THRASONIDES' *house*

The couple's departure into the house is of course expected from the moment of their arrival, and at 264 Thrasonides explicitly suggests that they go in: his lengthy delay on stage (259–69), besides covering the time needed for a costume change by one of the actors playing Demeas or Krateia to enable him to enter at 270 as Kleinias, reflects his concern and uncertainty over what may happen.

[13] See B(6) above.

[14] The attribution in O10 of πωc κτλ (269) to Getas is correctly overruled by GS ad loc.; see also Bain (1977) 133–4.

270. *Enter* KLEINIAS *and the* COOK *from the city*
Kleinias probably enters from the city, the usual place to hire a cook, talking to his companion who remains silent.[15] While the aspect of the plot concerned with Kleinias and this proposed party is now wholly unclear, Handley (1970) 13–14 remarks that the guest (270) is probably Demeas, and that this brief scene offers a different view of him following his emotional reunion with his daughter and the distressing discovery of his son's death.

275. *Exeunt* KLEINIAS *and* COOK *to* KLEINIAS' *house*
Kleinias orders the cook inside (274) and follows him. Handley (1970) 11 comparing this and the cook-scenes of *Dysk.* 393 ff. and *Aspis* 216 ff. observes that 'one effect of these three scenes, played as they are, is to bring the action down from a high point to which it has developed, and carry the act to a swift close on a new note'.

ΧΟΡΟΥ

276. *Enter* KLEINIAS *from his house*
Kleinias enters talking back to the old woman (280) and revealing that he has learnt about the depositing of the swords in his house and of Demeas' consequent behaviour (276–7). GS ad loc. remark that the length of his address—he may still be talking to the woman at 282a—may imply that she enters with him as a mute; in that case τί φῄϲ ('what are you telling me?', 276) is used as an indication of mid-conversational entry; compare *Dysk.* 50. However, since the old woman is not referred to again in what remains of the scene, and her silent presence might distract from what follows, it is more likely that Kleinias speaks back into the house, despite the unusual length of the address; for φῄϲ in an entrance talking back compare *Dysk.* 456. Kleinias' entrance motivation is not made explicit, although it may be assumed that he comes out to seek Demeas at the neighbour's house (277) when he discovers that he is not inside for the dinner; this may have been made clear by some words in the lacunose 281 or by a movement towards Thrasonides' doors.

[15] The cook is played by a mute whose silence allows a swift ending to the act: GS on 275 suggest that he must be mute due to the three-actor rule, but if one of the actors playing Demeas and Krateia could change during 259–69 to play Kleinias, what was to stop the other doing the same and playing a speaking cook, had Menander wished?

284. *Enter* GETAS *from* THRASONIDES' *house*
Kleinias delivers a door-noise announcement heralding Getas' arrival, and the slave bursts on to the stage with two oaths and an exclamatory phrase to express his emotion. In the following scenes Getas does not notice Kleinias until 324, despite the latter's attempts to catch his attention, so engrossed is he in his account of what he has witnessed indoors; see Blundell (180) 14–15. The excesses of the resulting farce indicate that this is a type-scene which may not have been entirely uncommon in Greek New Comedy; see the treatment by Bain (1977) 141–2. This may account for the complete lack of motivation for Getas' entrance, a point which in performance would no doubt be overlooked due to the pace and comedy of what follows.

[*Exit* KLEINIAS.]
[*Exit* GETAS]
At 341 εἰϲέρχομαι ('I'm going indoors') indicates that the conversation of Getas and Kleinias comes to an end as one of them leaves: since the monologue preserved from 360 indicates that Thrasonides is alone on stage, both the earlier participants in the scene must have left by this point, presumably into their respective houses.

[*Enter* THRASONIDES *from his house*]
The speaker of 360 who urges himself to be strong and to conceal his hurt is most likely to be Thrasonides following his rejection by Krateia, and this is almost certainly his monologue (cf. Blundell (1980) 69), although it is just possible that someone else is reporting his reaction with quoted speech; see GS on 324.

The text now becomes fragmentary, but when from 429 a more substantial amount is once more available, Getas' presence on stage is recorded by marginal Γε, and he announces to his dialogue partner[16] that 'they are giving the woman to you' (431). This, together with Demeas' entry to betrothe his daughter (443–4), indicates that Getas' dialogue partner is Thrasonides, who may have been present for some time already: his name is preserved in an unknown context at 419.

443. *Enter* DEMEAS *from* THRASONIDES' *house*
Getas delivers a door-noise announcement (442–3) and Demeas enters to betrothe his daughter; whether Krateia accompanies him is unclear from the fragments, but her presence is not necessary for the

[16] Movement away from the door is advised at 429a; for the same action before scenes of private dialogue cf. *Aspis* 457; *Sam.* 304.

ceremony;[17] GS on 443 consider some restorations of 443b which might shed light on this point, but note a variety of possible alternatives. In whatever way the half-line is supplemented, Demeas speaks only briefly before the betrothal; this suggests that he knows Thrasonides will be on-stage and comes out to find him.

466. *Exeunt omnes to* THRASONIDES' *house*

At 451 someone suggests going inside, but it is unclear whether anyone acts upon this. The final lines contain the traditional appeal for applause, on which see on *Dysk.* 969; the characters presumably enter Thrasonides' house to celebrate the betrothal.

[17] Cf. *Dysk.* 758, where Knemon's daughter probably leaves before her betrothal to Gorgias.

8
Perikeiromene

[*Enter* POLEMON]
[*Enter* SOSIAS]
[*Enter* GLYKERA]
[*Exeunt* POLEMON *and* SOSIAS *to the city,* GLYKERA *to the house*]
[*Enter* AGNOIA]

The goddess Agnoia, whose speech is in progress when the fragment begins, explicitly mentions two characters who have appeared on stage before her prologue: Glykera, the girl of the title (127–8), and a male character (157–8) who recounted to the audience what he had seen of the embrace which took place between her and her brother Moschion. This character's identity is lost in the gap at the end of 157 which has been variously supplemented, but GS 467–8 argue convincingly that it was Sosias, not Polemon, and that the slave recounted his story on-stage to his master. The most plausible reconstruction of the opening scenes based on these facts is proposed by Webster (1960) 5 and followed by Sandbach,[1] who modifies some points of detail: Sosias, sent on ahead of Polemon who is returning from abroad, meets his master and relates what he has seen, interpreting it as infidelity on Glykera's part. Presumably it is now that Glykera makes her appearance, perhaps summoned on stage to be questioned: Polemon in anger cuts off her hair[2] and leaves to drown his sorrows in the city (cf. GS on 175), accompanied by Sosias and leaving Glykera in his house.

Agnoia then enters when the stage is empty to explain what has happened and to put events into their proper context: as her prologue is delayed, the goddess may have appeared not on the stage but on the *skene* roof; see my note on *Aspis* 97.

171. *Exit* AGNOIA

[1] *Gnomon*, 39 (1967), 768; cf GS 468.

[2] Was the cutting done on stage? If so, the act would turn the audience strongly against the soldier (so GS, p. 468), but it may have been done inside the house and then reported: no conclusions can be drawn from the title of the play, since while some titles of this type are taken from actual scenes, e.g. *Epitrepontes* ('*The Men at Arbitration*'), on other occasions this is manifestly not the case, e.g. *Empimpramene* ('*The Girl who is Set on Fire*').

172. *Enter* SOSIAS *from the city*

Sosias' entrance monologue throws a new and significant light on Polemon by reporting his present grief and despondency which contrast with his earlier anger and violence.[3] The slave is unintroduced and unidentified, which may be proof that he is likely to have appeared earlier (see above): ἡμῖν ('our', 172) may be used to include the audience as Sosias reflects on the scenes he and they have just observed; see Bain (1977) 198–9. His motivation for entry is given late in the speech (178–9), after the important news of Polemon's change of heart; for this technique see my note on *Dysk.* 522 above.

181. *Enter* DORIS *from* POLEMON'*s house*

Doris, although unannounced (perhaps due to Sosias' absorption in his monologue),[4] is at once explicitly identified by the slave, which suggests that she has not appeared before; see Webster (1960) 5. She enters speaking back into the house to Glykera, delivering a line similar to *Dysk.* 879, which is also a passage where a new entrant reveals that he has been sent out with a definite mission to perform. Doris is going to Myrrhine's house, presumably to see whether she will accept her mistress; this mission, which is given no specific explanation, probably picks up an earlier formulation of the plan which the audience may have witnessed. Her attention is accordingly directed away from the stage, and she fails to see or hear Sosias (cf. GS on 181 ff.).

184. *Exit* SOSIAS *to* POLEMON'*s house*

Sosias explicitly announces his intention to leave with πορεύϲομαι ('I'll go', 184) and departs on his errand of 177ff.: his brief description of Doris (182–3) gives sufficient time for her to move away towards Myrrhine's door, allowing him to enter Polemon's house without attracting her attention.[5]

[3] On the deliberate effect of irony in the asyndeton of 172–3 see Blundell (1980) 36.

[4] See B(8) in the first part of this book.

[5] The dicola of the papyrus after παῖδεϲ (188) and αὐτόϲ (190) have been taken to imply a change of speaker, and GS on 188–90 suggest that Sosias, having collected the cloak, may re-enter to speak these lines. GS point out that they are more appropriate in Sosias' mouth: while he knows Polemon will hear of Glykera's distress, Doris can only suppose that he will. However, Sosias' entrance monologue has revealed that Polemon is himself grieving, and he knows that the soldier will feel no malicious pleasure in the news of Glykera's plight; this makes Doris the most likely speaker, since her most recent impression of Polemon is of his furious assault on her mistress. The dicola, then, indicate not change of speaker but of addressee, as the slave-woman indulges in soliloquy; cf. Bain (1977) 118–19.

Only an outline of the action in the following substantial lacuna can be reconstructed. Sosias returns to Polemon (cf. 334) and there seems little doubt that the transfer of Glykera to Myrrhine's house took place also: at 181 she is in Polemon's house, while in act ii she has taken refuge with Myrrhine. Gomme's suggestion[6] that she moves house during the choral interlude is without parallel in the extant Menander.[7]

266. *Exit* DAOS *to the city*
As the papyrus resumes at 261 Daos is speaking: παῖδεϲ (263a) followed by a dicolon in the papyrus may indicate that he has entered talking back to fellow slaves within and now turns to soliloquy; or alternatively he may be sending mutes indoors with Glykera's luggage (so Webster (1974) 169). In either case his original point of entry is probably from Myrrhine's house where he has learnt what has happened. He leaves to find Moschion with the news, his eagerness reflected by the verbal adjective (264; cf. on *Kith.* 66), and goes off presumably to the city, the most likely place for the young man to be found (although this is not made explicit in the surviving fragments). The chorus is announced (261–2) on its first apperance as was conventional (see on *Aspis* 249): as at *Dysk.* 232 and *Epitr.* 171 the speaker is already resolved to leave, and the approach of the revellers only supplements his motivation.

XOPOY

267. *Enter* MOSCHION *and* DAOS, *from the city*
Daos presumably returns with his master (cf. 264) and the couple enter in mid-conversation as Moschion warns his slave of the consequences of lying: Daos asserts the truth of the story he is supposed to have just told him, which he then summarizes for the audience's benefit (272–3). The effect of this entrance is of course primarily comic, as the audience is well aware that Glykera's transfer had nothing to do with Daos, and it serves to introduce a humorous scene where the swift interplay of dialogue is enhanced by the change to trochaic tetrameters (on whose

[6] *CQ* 30 (1936), 67.

[7] There appears in any case to have been a convention in Greek drama that a character should only enter from the direction to which he had last been seen to depart: Aris. *Poet.* 1455^{a}26 records the hostile reaction of the audience to a play of the fourth-century tragedian Karkinos which (according to T. B. L. Webster, *Hermes*, 82 (1954), 300) failed to observe this principle.

effect see GS on 267–93) as Daos attempts to maintain the illusion that Glykera has fallen for his master.

299. *Exit* DAOS *to* MYRRHINE'*s house*

Daos leaves in obedience to his master's orders of 295 ff. with the explicit πορεύcομαι ('I'll go', 298) spoken in acknowledgement to assure Moschion of his prompt compliance.[8] Moschion calls after him to speed him on his way.[9]

305. *Enter* DAOS *from* MYRRHINE'*s house*

Daos returns unannounced as Moschion compliments himself on his evident attractiveness to women. The slave's report of Glykera waiting like an hetaera (cf. GS on 305) comes as a surprise to the audience who may have expected that he would be unable, having seen the true state of affairs indoors, to maintain the fiction any longer: on the contrary, however, he manages to bolster Moschion's confidence even further.

310. *Exit* DAOS *to* MYRRHINE'*s house*

The slave leaves with fresh instructions for Moschion to make contact with the women, which he acknowledges (cf. on 299 above). The swift sequence of exits and entrances interlaced with Moschion's self-confident monologues, together with the audience's certainty of his imminent disillusionment, combine to produce a scene bordering on farce.

316. *Enter* DAOS *from* MYRRHINE'*s house*

Whereas his earlier re-entrance (310) was unannounced, on this occasion Moschion's attention is caught by the door noise which heralds Daos' arrival (316) and the announcement enables him to remark on the slave's manner before the dialogue begins. Moschion is surprised to see that Daos approaches fearfully (316–17); this is in marked contrast to his confident exit, and immediately shows the audience that the slave now has to reconcile the true state of affairs with the impression he has given his master.

It is worth noting that as much time as is covered by Moschion's monologue (311–17a) would be occupied merely by the conversation which Daos reports: however, Menander is not always careful to balance on- and off-stage time; see Blundell (1980) 26–7.

[8] On such acknowledgement see C(2) above.

[9] See C(3) above.

352a. *Exit* MOSCHION *to* MYRRHINE'*s house*

Moschion complies with Daos' suggestion that he should go indoors (348–9), encouraged by the slave's portrayal of Glykera as sophisticated and civilized rather than common (336–7). Under Körte's speaker-division adopted in the above interpretation, Daos repeats his instruction to Moschion at 351 and his master, who is now mollified, agrees and leaves. This is preferable to the division of the OCT where it is Moschion who instructs Daos at 351, and the slave agrees yet remains on stage: while in comedy a slave is under no compulsion to obey his master's orders (cf. Bain (1981) 44–7), J. C. B. Lowe[10] argues convincingly that is is more appropriate for Daos in his predicament to send his master off with no intention of accompanying him. Daos remains on stage with one and a half lines of monologue to round off the scene; Blundell (1980) 50 collects some parallel examples.

354. *Enter* SOSIAS *from the city*

On entering Sosias at once explains his motivation: again his master has sent him ostensibly on an errand, but in fact to report back on what is happening. As at 172, by throwing more light on Polemon's grief, the entrance monologue portrays the soldier as an increasingly sympathetic character in preparation for the eventual reconciliation with Glykera. Sosias is unannounced, yet when he leaves Daos has clearly become aware of him and believes from what he has heard that Polemon has returned to the country (cf. GS on 361): Daos fails to see Sosias when he enters as he is engrossed in his own thoughts (cf. on 181 above), but may be alerted to his presence by the sound of his voice, perhaps indicating this to the audience by a gesture; cf. *Epitr.* 430ff. and note. As Sosias starts to speak the metre reverts to the iambic trimeter, a shift which seems to denote a change of mood as the previous farcical master–servant scenes are followed by Sosias' more serious discovery of, and reaction to, what has happened.

360. *Exit* SOSIAS *to* POLEMON'*s house*

Sosias, whose exit has been expected since his appearance, leaves without an explicit exit-line but with an emotional exclamation (360b)[11] which rounds off the lines emphasizing Polemon's present distress (358–60; cf. GS ad loc.). Daos' monologue covers the time needed for his business indoors; cf. Blundell (1980) 26.

[10] *BICS* 20 (1973), 103.

[11] For further examples see C(5) n. 105 above.

366. *Enter* SOSIAS *from* POLEMON'*s house, followed by* DORIS
Sosias bursts on to the stage shouting back at the slaves indoors, and his words reveal at once that he has learnt of Glykera's departure: his anger is clear from his abuse of the household (365b),his incredulous repetition of their offence (366–7), and from Daos' comment on his manner ὀϱγιζόμενος ('in anger', 368). Sosias evidently storms across the stage to Myrrhine's house causing Daos to withdraw from the door, and this withdrawal together with Sosias' preoccupation prevents him from noticing Daos until approached (373): some indication of movement by the slave in the lacunose ending of 368 would clarify the action; with the attractive restoration ὑπα]π̣ο̣[ϲτήϲομαι ('I'll stand back') GS ad loc. compare *Sam.* 368.

The first explicit sign of Doris' presence comes when she addresses Sosias as Daos is leaving (376b). The phrasing of 402–3 shows that she has come from Polemon's house (cf. Bain (1977) 121 n. 4 (ii)) and the most convenient point for this entrance is at 366 or shortly afterwards, where, in following Sosias out, her reason for entry would be perfectly clear; see GS on 366. A disadvantage would be her silent[12] and unremarked presence during the ensuing confrontation of Sosias and Daos (372–97a) but this is perhaps less awkward than an unexplained entrance at some point during the scene, also in silence.

384.
Various attempts have been made to reconcile the fragmentary traces in 384 with intelligible and coherent restorations of meaning and action. Of these attempts the most satisfactory yet is the proposal of L. Koenen,[13] based on the suggestion of J. R. Rea:[14] π̣ϱ̣[όϲ]ελθ', ἄνθϱωφ' [ὁ π]αϱιών—οἴχετ̣[αι ('come here, you passer-by—he's gone'). Rea argues that Sosias, having accused Daos of harbouring a free woman against the will of her guardian (376) calls to a passer-by for help, citing evidence for such a practice.[15] However, the passer-by does not stop (cf. *Sam.* 547), and he may not even have appeared on-stage: either a mute may have walked across the stage or Sosias may have called to someone supposed to be out of sight of the audience in the wings.

[12] Jensen and Sudhaus interpret a marginal note at 377–8 as Δ]Ω i.e. ΔΩΡΙϹ, but the reading is dubious; see GS on 377–8 and F. H. Sandbach, *ZPE* 40 (1980), 50–1.

[13] *ZPE* 16 (1975), 133.

[14] *ZPE* 16 (1975), 128–9; note that Rea reads πάϱ]ελθ', not π̣ϱ̣[όϲ]ελθ'.

[15] Further evidence is cited by D. Bain, *ZPE* 49 (1982), 42.

397. *Exit* DAOS *to* MYRRHINE'*s house*

Daos leaves with an explicit exit-line and an insult (396). Sosias' rage is evident from his violent threat against Doris when she addresses him.

[*Exit* DORIS *presumably to* POLEMON'*s house*]
[*Exit* SOSIAS *to the city*]

[ΧΟΡΟΥ]

[*Enter* POLEMON, SOSIAS, HABROTONON, *and* MUTE SLAVES *from the city*]
[*Enter* PATAIKOS]

In the lacuna which extends across the act-break the minimum necessary movements require Doris to leave, presumably back to Polemon's house, and Sosias to go to summon Polemon from the city: at the start of the following act, where between twenty and forty lines are missing (see GS 501) the slave returns with his master, Habrotonon, and some mute assistants (477) with the intention of seizing Glykera by force. Whether Pataikos accompanies them or enters separately is unclear from the surviving text where at 467 the characters are involved in an argument when the fragment resumes; but GS 501 favour the view that ἐκεῖθεν ἥκει ('he came from there', 467) is best understood if Pataikos does not arrive with Polemon, and he may simply enter from one of the sides, perhaps summoned by Doris in the now-lost ending of act ii; so Gomme *apud* GS 501. An entrance from his house is most unlikely as this would involve three private houses on stage, a situation unparalleled in the extant Menander.

485. *Exeunt* HABROTONON, SOSIAS, *and the* MUTE ASSISTANTS *to* POLEMON'*s house*

Pataikos urges Polemon to dismiss his raiding-party (476–7) and the soldier may comply with a silent gesture of dismissal at 477 which prompts Sosias' objection κακῶϲ γε πολεμεῖϲ ('this is a poor war you're waging!'):[16] as Polemon wavers in the face of Sosias' complaints (479–80), Pataikos himself repeats the instruction to the slave (481). With the explicit ἀπέρχομαι ('I'm going', 481b) Sosias turns to address Habrotonon and succeeds in offending her with his coarse humour, causing her to turn (484b) to go to Polemon's house (cf.

[16] For the text see H. Lloyd-Jones, *ZPE* 15 (1974), 211.

476). In the following dialogue there is no hint that Polemon and Pataikos are not alone on stage and as a result Habrotonon will be followed by the mute assistants and by Sosias himself, still drunkenly questioning her.[17]

525. *Exeunt* POLEMON *and* PATAIKOS *to* POLEMON'*s house*
Polemon eventually persuades Pataikos to accompany him to view Glykera's finery, an idea which occurred to him originally at 516–17: after an initial and sensible reluctance Pataikos gives in to what is, as GS on 516 comment, a pointless proposal that reveals Polemon's naïvety, and in accordance with the repeated requests (517, 518, 525) follows the soldier off with an explicit exit-line which is designed to reassure the eager Polemon.[18]

526. *Enter* MOSCHION *from* MYRRHINE'*s house*
Moschion enters as soon as Polemon and Pataikos have left, with an insult directed at them (526): his bravado has a comic effect since he has obviously waited for them to be out of earshot before entering. He emerges surprisingly defiant and as yet undisillusioned over his chances with Glykera: this is quickly revealed to be due to his failure to approach his mother or the girl inside. No motivation is given for his entrance in the preserved part of the monologue, but he may have come out to consider what to do, and this may have been made explicit in the lost sections, since motivation in entrance monologues is not uncommonly held back until the end of the speech; see on 172 above.

Since Moschion knows not only who is on stage but also when it is safe to enter, he must have been eavesdropping on the conversation: there is no evidence in the text of when this is supposed to begin (although his knowledge of Sosias (531) who left at 485 shows he has been listening for some time) and Moschion may simply become visible for the first time when he enters at 526; a similar device of

[17] Sandbach (1975) 197 n. 1 has retracted the proposal of GS on 485 that Sosias remains asleep on stage, a view based on the supposition that οὑτοσί (531) requires his actual presence. This deictic, like ὅδε, does not necessarily imply the physical presence of the subject, only that he is 'present to the speaker's thought' (H. Lloyd-Jones, *CR* 15 (1965), 241); see also the bibliography at R. L. Hunter, *Eubulus* (Cambridge, 1983), 106 and compare οὑτοσί at *Aspis* 139 and *Geo.* 63. At *Perik.* 531 Moschion could have accompanied the word with a gesture towards Polemon's house; so J. Rea, *ZPE* 16 (1975), 131. The original proposal of GS would in any case involve a breach of the three-actor rule since at 526 the third speaking actor who plays Sosias from 467 is needed to enter as Moschion as soon as Polemon and Pataikos have left; cf. Blundell (1980) 15.

[18] On this device see C(2) above.

unseen eavesdropping is used in *Dysk.* (821) and probably in *Epitr.* (lost sections of act iv).

[ΧΟΡΟΥ]

The lacuna 550–708 is too lengthy for a reconstruction on any but the broadest lines; for a detailed examination see GS 511–13. When the fragment resumes Pataikos and Glykera are on stage engaged in an argument, and Körte[19] is almost certainly correct to suppose that the act began with an entrance of the two in mid-conversation, creating a dramatic opening concealing the probable lack of motivation for leaving the house; for these effects cf. *Dysk.* 784; *Epitr.* 714.[20]

752. *Exit* MUTE SLAVE *to* POLEMON'*s house*
Presumably a mute attendant leaves in response to Pataikos' order to summon Doris. In the extant earlier portions of the act no other reference is made to any mute attendants on stage, although the lack of clarity may be due to the lacunose text; for some suggestions on the whereabouts of the mute see GS on 751.[21]

754. *Enter* DORIS *from* POLEMON'*s house*
Doris enters in distress (758) in response to the summons (752); on the direction of her entry see Bain (1977) 121 n. 4.

758. *Exit* DORIS *to* POLEMON'*s house*
In the following fragmentary lines Doris, who is ordered in (755–6) on her errand (on which see GS 756), presumably leaves at 758 where τί κλάεις, ἀθλία; ('why are you weeping, poor woman?') is certainly addressed to her and is probably a reproof rather than a genuine question; see Bain (1977) 121–3, who also discusses the reasons for her distress.

[*Re-enter* DORIS *from* POLEMON'*s house with the tokens*]
[*Exit* DORIS *to* POLEMON'*s house*]
After the gap 760–8 the papyrus resumes as Pataikos is examining the birth tokens. Since there is no sign of Doris' presence in the text, and under the three-actor rule the third speaking actor must enter as Moschion at 774, Doris enters and departs in the lacuna having carried out her errand; see Bain (1977) 114 n. 3, 121–3.

19 *Menander* (Leipzig, 1955), p. xxxiv.
20 See further B(6) above.
21 On mutes generally see A(2) above.

774. *Enter* MOSCHION *from the side*

The reasons for regarding 774ff. as an entrance monologue rather than an aside from a position of eavesdropping have been stated by Bain (1977) 113–14 and need no repetition. Moschion's direction of entry is not clear from the text, presumably because of the substantial earlier lacunae in which his departure was witnessed by the audience; but he is perhaps most likely to enter from one of the sides, the city or the country, having left earlier to ponder what has happened; Bain (1977) 201 compares *Geo.* 20. Moschion is unannounced as the couple on stage are as engrossed in their thoughts[22] as he is in his, and so there is an initial stage of mutual unawareness: when Moschion next speaks (783) he has observed the others and withdraws to eavesdrop. Probably he is alerted to their presence by the sound of Pataikos continuing the dialogue (779) and may indicate this to the audience by a gesture; cf. *Epitr.* 442 and note.

[XOPOY]

On the substantial lacuna see GS 525–6.

982. POLEMON [*to Doris*]. Excellent news! Go inside. [*Turns away as he dismisses her, and Doris goes off into Myrrhine's house. Unaware of her departure, he continues*] I'll make you a free woman tomorrow, Doris. But listen to what you must say. [*Turns back to face her and realizes she has gone*] She's gone indoors!

Polemon sends Doris in to Glykera and she leaves in silence, presumably either at this point or after his promise to set her free (982–3), since she does not wait to hear his further instructions (983–4) and the soldier acknowledges that she has gone in (984).[23] As he does not notice the point at which the slave-woman leaves, Polemon presumably turns away from her early in his speech (981–2) and turns back at 984 to find her gone. Doris' direction of exit can be inferred from the fact that Glykera is not in Polemon's house (since at 1003 the soldier leaves in that direction to avoid Pataikos and his daughter who enter from another house at 1006; the most straightforward view is that the couple come on from Myrrhine's house). The suggestion[24] that Pataikos' house is represented on-stage and Glykera is there with her

[22] See B(8) above.

[23] See further C(5)(*b*) above.

[24] Körte (op. cit. n. 19 above), *actio* on 406.

father introduces an unnecessary third private house on stage, on the unlikelihood of which see 467–8 above.

989. *Enter* DORIS *from* MYRRHINE'*s house*
Polemon eagerly asks the slave-woman for news: it may be that this scene of a lover sending a slave inside to observe and negotiate with his beloved was intended to recall the events of act ii involving Moschion and Daos.

1003. *Exit* POLEMON *to his house*
The exact circumstances of Polemon's withdrawal are now uncertain due to the fragmentary state of the text. On hearing that someone is about to come out (1002) he leaves the stage, and Doris' reaction suggests that he takes the door noise as his cue (1003–4). Polemon is plainly nervous and GS on 1003 comment that the scene has now become farcical; however, the lines leading up to his departure are of little aid in understanding the action. At 1001 the papyrus offers αγετε [. . .] ξ[: here Polemon may order the girl Glykera to be brought out, reading γε ἔξω τὴν κόρην ('bring the girl out') with G. M. Browne,[25] or he may ask for help in pleading his case, reading προ]ξ[ενεῖτέ μοι ('plead my case for me') with Sandbach.[26] The identity of the person whose entrance is predicted at 1002 is lost in the lacuna, if indeed it was given: GS on 1003 discuss restorations of an announcement of either withdrawal by Polemon or arrival of Pataikos. In the latter case Polemon leaves as he is unwilling to meet his old friend in his new role as Glykera's father: in the former, he is too nervous to meet his beloved (which would rule out Browne's restoration of 1001). However, a positive dramatic gain of Polemon's withdrawal followed by Doris is that Pataikos and Glykera enter an empty stage, allowing Glykera's reconciliation with her lover to be stressed in the lines 1006–9 before dialogue begins with Polemon.

1005. *Exit* DORIS *to* POLEMON'*s house*
Doris leaves following the soldier with an explicit exit-line and statement of motivation (to assist Polemon): see also above.

1006. *Enter* PATAIKOS *and* GLYKERA *from* MYRRHINE'*s house*
The couple's entrance has been prepared by Doris (1002) and by door noise (1004). The evidence for regarding Glykera as a mute role in the

25 *BICS* 21 (1974), 53.
26 GS, Addenda, p. 745.

following scene (despite the speaker attributions in the papyrus which appear to give 1021–2a and 1023 to her by means of the abbreviation κε) is set out by Sandbach[27] who observes that to give Glykera a speaking part would not only breach the three-actor rule, unless there are improbably swift changes of costume or an unwelcome pause in the rapid action between 1005 and 1006, but would also place an unjustified confidence in the apparent speaker-attributions of the papyrus which are, most probably, due to the conjecture of a reader unlikely to have had any authority for his views. If Sandbach is correct, an impression of an entrance in mid-conversation is made as Pataikos refers to Glykera's supposed words just before entry, thereby concealing her mute status.[28]

1010. *Enter* POLEMON *from his house*

Polemon enters and presumably pre-empts the mute slave who is sent at 1009 to fetch him, and who may have accompanied Pataikos and Glykera from the house, or simply have been present in the background.[29] The soldier's appearance is most timely and allows the betrothal to proceed without delay, but his explanation for his absence, that he has been carrying out a sacrifice, is at variance with his earlier exit (1003) which was brought on by timidity. As observed above, the scene is now farcical, and Polemon may in fact have been seen to have been eavesdropping at his door during the last few lines, having reappeared there after Doris leaves to follow him in: his nervousness over Pataikos' and Glykera's attitude to him would be dispelled by the former's speech on entry, and he may take the order to the mute (1009) as his cue to come forward, explaining his absence by seizing on the suggestion of Doris at 993–4. However, much of the difficulty here is due to the lacunose state of the text.

[*Enter* MOSCHION*?*]

[*Exeunt omnes to* POLEMON'*s house*]

Only two speaking actors are on stage from 1010, and Glykera, the third character, is played by a mute (see above): this leaves the third speaking actor free to enter in another role in the final scenes; compare my comments on the end of *Epitr.* above. It may be that

[27] *PCPhS* 13 (1967), 40–1; GS 529–30.

[28] On this device see B(6) above.

[29] On the apparently conventional lack of clarity over the whereabouts of mutes used for such tasks see A(2) above.

Moschion entered and agreed to the marriage proposed for him (1025–6).[30] The play will end with the traditional celebrations of the betrothal, presumably in Polemon's house.

[30] The stage direction in the papyrus at 1024 πολεμειcιcι appears to be a mistake, as Polemon would hardly now abandon his bride and prospective father-in-law so abruptly merely to carry out a sacrifice.

9

Samia

[I. *Enter* MOSCHION, *presumably from* DEMEAS' *house*]

The papyrus begins as Moschion is describing his relationship with his father, some eleven lines from the start of the play. His motivation for entry is now lost in the lacuna but C. Dedoussi[1] suggests reasonably enough that before addressing the audience Moschion may have begun his speech with an invocation of some deity and compares Plaut. *Merc.* 3ff. for this common practice of lovers: 'non ego item facio ut alios in comoediis | vi vidi amoris facere, qui aut Nocti aut Dii | aut Soli aut lunae miserias narrant suas' ('I won't do what I've seen others do in comedies under the influence of love, telling their sorrows to Night or Day or the sun or the moon').

[*Exit* MOSCHION *to the harbour*]

Moschion's exit motivation is lost in the gap; but as his next appearance is from the harbour with Parmenon, and his speech (53) prepares the audience for his father's arrival home, he may announce that he is going there to find out news about the ship, and may reveal that he has stationed Parmenon there for that very purpose; cf. Blume (1974) 20 and GS 551 who compare Plaut. *Stitch.* 151–2.[2]

[*Enter* CHRYSIS, *presumably from* DEMEAS' *house*]

Since all but one and a half lines of the scene in the lacuna featuring Chrysis are now lost, it is impossible to be sure of her direction of entry or motivation; the suggestion of Blume (1974) 21 that she enters from Demeas' house on her way to chat with her neighbour (cf. 34–5) is as likely as any. She appears to have delivered a monologue on an empty stage:[3] the plural πρὸς ἡμᾶς (59) is more likely, on the analogy of the identical phrase at 40, to mean 'to our house' than to imply that Chrysis is accompanied by a mute attendant who is not mentioned in the remaining fragments of the scene; see GS on 59.

[1] *Entretiens Hardt*, 16 (1970), 176.

[2] Contrast R. L. Hunter, *MH* 37 (1980), 223 who doubts the comparison with *Stichus*.

[3] It is unlikely that in the lacuna there was a contact between Chrysis and Moschion, as the latter is unaware of the former's presence at 61; see Blundell (1980) 44 n. 19.

61. *Enter* MOSCHION *and* PARMENON *from the harbour*
Chrysis apparently delivers a visual announcement of the new entrants who are approaching 'in a hurry' (59) and may move back to eavesdrop (60) although a movement to withdraw is not (unlike e.g. *Geo.* 32–3) made explicit. Moschion and Parmenon are too engrossed to notice her and enter in mid-conversation, an effect conveyed by the initial apistetic question (61) and the characteristic brief summary for the audience's benefit of the conversation so far (62–3).[4] Chrysis makes contact at 69 and is swiftly incorporated into the dialogue; on Parmenon's reaction to her presence (70a) see Bain (1977) 161.

[*Exeunt* CHRYSIS *and* PARMENON, *presumably to* DEMEAS' *house*]
When the fragments resume at 88 Moschion is delivering a monologue on his predicament, and there is no sign that he is not alone on stage. Chrysis and Parmenon appear to leave in the gap after 85, probably so that Chrysis may await the return of Demeas, accompanied by Parmenon who is to be found in the house at 189.

95. *Exit* MOSCHION *to the country*
At the end of his soliloquy Moschion declares he will go 'to some deserted spot' (94) to practise his speech, and this is almost certainly the country; see Blume (1974) 33. For a similar scene-ending compare *Geo.* 20–1 where, as here, a conversation follows which throws new light on the previous speaker's circumstances.

96. *Enter* DEMEAS *and* NIKERATOS, *with* ATTENDANTS, *from the harbour*[5]
Demeas' opening words, which constitute an entry in mid-conversation (note the connective οὐκοῦν) even though there is no

[4] See B(6) in the first part of this book.

[5] This passage suggests that country and harbour are conceived as lying on opposite sides of the stage (contrast the suggestion of GS, p. 12) to avoid an unwanted meeting of Moschion with his returning father and neighbour in the wings. The significance of the side entrances in the various periods of Greek drama has been much debated but remains uncertain: for discussion see K. Rees, *AJPh* 32 (1911), 377–402; Flickinger (1936) 233–4; Taplin (1977) 450–1. In view of the present passage it is tempting to compare the actual topographical situation of the theatre of Dionysos at Athens where harbour and city were found to the spectators' right and open country to their left, and to suppose these directions to have been adopted for New-Comedy plays set in Athens; cf. Handley (1965) 129; Newiger (1979) 490–1. However, there is evidence from Euripides that exits and entrances of characters who must be supposed not to meet could occur simultaneously using the same *parodos* without awkwardness: see the remarks of A. M. Dale, *Euripides'* Alcestis (Oxford, 1954), on 860; N. C. Hourmouziades, *Production and Imagination in Euripides* (Athens, 1965), 133 n. 2; Flickinger (1936) 234–5. If such a convention did exist, the present passage of *Samia* provides no evidence for the significance of Menander's side entrances.

hint as to what may have preceded them, are addressed both to Nikeratos and to the entourage,[6] and the introductory exchange is used to characterize the two old men; see Sandbach (1970) 121–1. The entrance, featuring Demeas' fantastic explanation of the lack of sunshine in Pontos and Nikeratos' credulous acceptance of it (110–12a) marks a change of mood from Moschion's earnest and anxious departure at 95: consequently the important fact, introduced almost in passing, that the young man's marriage to his beloved has been agreed by the two fathers surprises the audience and catches them unawares.

105. *Exeunt* ATTENDANTS *severally to* DEMEAS' *and* NIKERATOS' *houses*
For the abuse of the slave slow to obey orders (105b) see *Dysk.* 441.

[*Exuent* DEMEAS *and* NIKERATOS, *presumably to their respective houses*]
118b may be an exit-line, but there is scope in the scene for further discussion between the old men over the arrangements for the marriage; see GS on 118. The last to remain on stage would presumably leave with a conventional remark on the approach of the first chorus; see on *Aspis* 249.

[ΧΟΡΟΥ]

[*Enter* DEMEAS *from his house*]
[*Enter* MOSCHION *from the country*]
When the papyrus resumes, Moschion is finishing a monologue describing his dreams of his marriage, and at 127 notices Demeas who is already present but who appears not to have seen his son: Blundell (1980) 25 suggests that Moschion begins to pace about at the start of the line as he begins a new section of his speech and in the course of the movement notices his father. This is preferable to the suggestion of GS on 126 that ἦν ἀβέλτεϱοϲ ('I was foolish', 126) is spoken by Demeas and attracts the young man's attention.

Demeas may have entered at the beginning of the act to relate, perhaps in a monologue similar to that which begins act iii, his discovery that Chrysis has a child which she claims is her own (cf. 130–1): he is so engrossed in indignation that he fails to observe Moschion arriving back from his trip of 94–5. It is unlikely that Demeas withdraws to eavesdrop on his son, as he shows no sign when

[6] Blume (1974) 33 plausibly suggests that Demeas is accompanied by a large number of slaves, Nikeratos perhaps by only one, creating an instant visual impression of their respective statuses.

approached of having heard what Moschion has said, as the latter fears (129).

162. *Exit* MOSCHION *to the city*
The exchanges leading up to Moschion's departure are obscured by the lacunose text, but if the supplements and part-attributions of *OCT* are correct (on which see GS on 156–9) Moschion's eagerness to fetch his bride is checked by Demeas (158–60) and he leaves to the city (cf. 431–2) while the proper arrangements are made for the wedding, realizing that his presence would be inappropriate (161–2). West proposed ἀλλ' ἀπέρχομαι ('but I'm off!') to complete 162 with an explicit exit indication, and this is surely along the right lines.

[*Enter* NIKERATOS *from his house*]
The papyrus resumes at a point apparently just before contact is made between Demeas and Nikeratos with the greeting at 169. The circumstances of Nikeratos' entry in the preceding lines are unclear: despite the arrangement made between the old men earlier (118) the surviving words do not appear to fit a door-knocking sequence as there is no trace of the characteristic phrases associated elsewhere with such an action.[7] The simplest solution is to suppose that following Demeas' monologue (163–4) Nikeratos enters to find Demeas, perhaps wondering at the delay in summoning him (cf. GS on 167): Demeas may announce his neighbour's entrance and express an intention to tackle him at 167–8.

190. *Enter* PARMENON *from* DEMEAS' *house*
The slave enters in response to Demeas' summons (189) and is presumably present to receive the orders in the next line.

195. *Exit* PARMENON *to* DEMEAS' *house*
The slave leaves in obedience to his instructions, having delayed carrying out the orders in a display of characteristic curiosity (cf. on 664).

198a. *Exit* NIKERATOS *to his house*

198b. *Enter* PARMENON *form* DEMEAS' *house*
Parmenon enters carrying the basket with which he returns at 297, talking back to the household who may be imagined to be surprised at the sudden order to prepare for the wedding. GS on 195 suggest that

[7] See above, ch. 1 n. 11.

these words are heard from within the house and that the actual entrance does not occur until 202, but it is equally possible that Parmenon may dawdle in the doorway while Demeas, wrapped up in his own thoughts, speaks 200–2a: he then notices the slave, scolds him, and sends him on his way (202–3).

[*Exit* PARMENON *to the city*]

[*Enter* NIKERATOS *from his house*]
[*Exit* NIKERATOS *to the city*]
[*Exit* DEMEAS *to his house*]
Nikeratos must reappear and follow Parmenon (cf. 196b–8a): Demeas may then be left on stage with a few words of soliloquy; see Blume (1974) 76.

[ΧΟΡΟΥ]

[*Enter* DEMEAS *from his house*]
When the papyrus resumes Demeas is delivering an account in monologue form of what he has just heard indoors: probably only a few words from the start are missing. No explicit reason is given in what survives for his appearance on stage, but so gripping is the speech with its implications of the misunderstanding involved that if no motivation was given, this would go unnoticed. Demeas enters in a calm and sober manner (cf. 262–4) and his monologue, in which the crucial information which he has learnt is kept back for forty lines (see GS 564), increases in emotion towards its climax at 279.

283. *Enter* PARMENON *leading the* COOK *and his* ASSISTANT(S) *from the city*
Demeas delivers a visual announcement of Parmenon, remarking on his timely arrival:[8] the slave is leading the cook and an indeterminate number of slaves who carry his equipment. Demeas presumably withdraws so as not to be seen at 282, although the movement is not explicitly indicated. Parmenon and the cook enter in mid-conversation with clear references to what is supposed to have been said prior to entry (λαλῶν, 'chattering', 285; cf. 287–8), and the instantly recognizable jokes of the traditional cook-scene provide a comic element after Demeas' long and serious speech.[9]

[8] For further examples see B(1) n. 39 above.
[9] Cf. C. Dedoussi, *Entretiens Hardt*, 16 (1970), 31.

295a. *Exeunt* COOK *and* ASSISTANT(S) *to* DEMEAS' *house*
The exchanges of Parmenon and the cook degenerate into abuse, and the slave orders the group inside.

Parmenon is probably at the door following the others in when Demeas calls him back (295b): as a result the slave in unaware of the identity of the speaker until he turns round to see his master. The interrupted movement to leave introduces the important scene where Demeas questions the slave,[10] and the suspense is heightened as the confrontation is momentarily delayed while Parmenon is ordered to go and leave his basket indoors (297: an errand which allows him to flee unencumbered at 325).

297. *Exit* PARMENON to DEMEAS' *house*
On the manner of this exit under orders see GS on 297ff. who discuss the tone of ἀγαθῆι τύχηι.

301. *Enter* PARMENON *from* DEMEAS' *house*
The slave's re-entry is given a door announcement (300b–1a) and Sandbach,[11] noting the use of πλήccειν instead of the more usual ψοφεῖν, plausibly suggests that the choice of verb, along with the orders he gives to Chrysis as he enters talking back, reflects his confidence, which is about to be shattered by Demeas. Parmenon's carefree attitude expressed in this exit and re-entrance is a source of great irony as it stands in stark contrast to Demeas' anger and determination to learn the truth from him. Before the subject of Demeas' fury is broached, he leads the slave away from the door (304): for a similar movement from the door before private dialogue see *Aspis* 457; *Mis.* 429.

At 321 Demeas calls for a strap but it is unlikely that a slave enters in response to the request; see on *Dysk.* 500.

324. *Exit* PARMENON *to the side*
The slave leaves presumably at a run, but his direction is unclear: there is no clue where he has been when he returns at 641.

Demeas' order at 325a is probably not acted upon, nor addressed to any specific person; see Austin (1970) and GS ad loc.

357. *Enter the* COOK *from* DEMEAS' *house*
The cook emerges in search of Parmenon with a brief entrance monologue which makes his motivation explicit (357–9a), remaining

[10] On such delayed exits see C(4) above.
[11] See Sandbach (1970) 33; GS on 300–1.

in the doorway where he is pushed aside at 359–60: παῖ (360, 362) is probably simply exclamatory and does not imply either a call for Parmenon or the presence of a mute assistant; see GS on 360. The cook shows no sign on entry of having seen Demeas, who may be supposed to be away to one side of the stage (cf. 304) and so not immediately conspicuous; but even if the cook does notice him he has no reason to recognize the old man as the master of the house. This entrance serves two purposes: first to cover the off-stage time required for Demeas to expel Chrysis and secondly to enable the cook to provide a comic dimension to the predominantly serious expulsion scene which follows.[12]

360. *Exit* DEMEAS *to his house*

Demeas rushes inside pushing the cook out of the way as he puts into action his resolve of 350–4: he is silent during the entrance monologue (357–9), engrossed in his own thoughts, and presumably only sees the cook when he turns to go in at 359b; see Blume (1974) 129. The cook's reaction gives an alternative and comic view of Demeas' important exit, determined to drive Chrysis out for reasons the audience knows are based on a misapprehension: to him Demeas is only 'some crazy old man' (361), and his exit acknowledgement (361) reflects the speed of the departure.[13]

369. *Enter* DEMEAS *and* CHRYSIS *with the* BABY *and a mute* NURSE[14] *from* DEMEAS' *house*

Demeas emerges driving Chrysis and the others before him, his instruction ἄπιθι ('be gone!', 369) apparently in continuation of the violent scene within (οὔκουν ἀκούεις, 'Didn't you hear me?', 369; cf. 62). The cook delivers a door announcement (366–7) where the choice of verb may reflect the force with which the door is flung open; cf. on 301 above. This continues the impression of mayhem within conveyed earlier by the off-stage shouting interpreted for the audience (364)[15] and the cook takes the door noise as his cue to withdraw and observe.

[12] See F. H. Sandbach, *Gnomon*, 39 (1967), 241: 'the cook's futile interruptions when Demeas turns Chrysis away keep the scene on the level of comedy: it is ridiculous to be diverted from high emotions by an irrelevant annoyance.' Cf. GS on 368 and 398.

[13] For such use of an exit acknowledgement see C(5)(*b*).

[14] Cf. 373. The nurse does not, apparently, accompany Chrysis in the second expulsion (569–70) but is probably not a sufficiently important character for this to worry the audience. Her presence here contributes to the effect of Chrysis' complete rejection.

[15] For a parallel interpretation of off-stage noises cf. 553 below and *Dysk.* 648–9.

390. *Exit* COOK *to* DEMEAS' *house*

The cook leaves with the explicit εἰcέρχομαι ('I'm going indoors') in an attempt to calm Demeas' violent anger (388).[16] On the one hand his presence is no longer needed in the scene (cf. Blume (1974) 151) and on the other his exit some lines before that of Demeas is required since under the three-actor rule the actor playing the cook must change to enter as Nikeratos at 399: even so it may have been necessary to provide a few extra moments at 398–9 for the transfer from *skene*-building to side entrance, perhaps by some silent business on Chrysis' part; see GS on 416.

398. *Exit* DEMEAS *to his house*

Demeas departs without an explicit exit-line, but his parting word ἕcταθι ('stay there!') which is prompted perhaps by a movement by Chrysis towards him, is made emphatic by its position: the effect is instantly recognizable to the audience who can see that it is accompanied by an exit, but is initially problematic for the reader who can only subsequently infer that Demeas has in fact left.[17] Demeas may bolt the door noisily as he goes in (416; cf. GS ad loc.), which stresses Chrysis' exclusion: she is left abandoned lamenting her plight, and some silent action to convey her distress further may provide some time for costume changes behind the scenes; see on 390.

399. *Enter* NIKERATOS *with a sheep from the city*

The sight of a man leading a sheep on to the stage constituted a familiar comic scene (cf. Handley (1965) on *Dysk.* 393 (which opens with the same first three words) and Blume (1974) 153), and Nikeratos' entrance marks a lowering of the emotional tone after Demeas' furious tirade and Chrysis' lament; see Blundell (1980) 39. Indeed, so occupied is Nikeratos with the animal that it is not until 405 that he notices Chrysis, perhaps attracted by the sound of her crying (406).

420. *Exeunt* NIKERATOS, *the sheep,* CHRYSIS, *the baby, and the* NURSE *to* NIKERATOS' *house*

Nikeratos instructs Chrysis to follow him indoors and leaves encouraging her: his diagnosis of the cause of Demeas' behaviour, the visit to Pontos (416–17), illustrates his simple-mindedness.

[16] On such acknowledgement of exit instructions see C(2) above.

[17] On this passage in particular and the effect in general see C(5)(*a*) above.

ΧΟΡΟΥ

421. *Enter* NIKERATOS *from his house*
Nikeratos appears addressing his first line back to his wife indoors, and explicitly giving his motivation: he is going to tackle Demeas over what has happened, and παρατενεῖϲ ('you'll be the death of me') indicates the uproar which has resulted from Chrysis' experiences, an uproar which he further describes at 426. The metre has changed to trochaic tetrameters, and Blume (1974) 158 suggests that the use of what seems to have been a livelier metre allows Nikeratos to deliver his lines with an energy which suits his indignation.

428. *Enter* MOSCHION *from the city*
The dramatic convenience of Moschion's appearance at this point distracts the audience from the lack of motivation. He makes clear in his entrance monologue that he is simply whiling away his time before the wedding (see Blundell (1980) 40) and as yet knows nothing of recent events: his meeting with Parmenon in the agora (431–2) took place during the slave's shopping trip (189–92), not after his flight from Demeas (325). Both Moschion and Nikeratos are engrossed in their respective monologues so that the youth's entrance is unannounced, and he fails to observe the old man's presence: at what point Nikeratos becomes aware of Moschion's presence is uncertain, but he is probably seen to notice him at some point during the brief entrance monologue and greets him at 430b.

440. *Enter* DEMEAS *from his house*
Demeas bursts out of the house in a fury, with sufficient abruptness to cut Nikeratos off in mid-sentence:[18] like his neighbour at the start of the act, he too emerges talking back, in this case to his household (ὑμῶν, 440), with a speech reflecting the uproar within; see Blundell (1980) 40. As he delivers his angry threats, Moschion and Nikeratos may engage in some kind of dumb show to suggest a continuing conversation and an awareness of Demeas (see the discussion by Bain (1974) 168) although this is not explicit in the text and Blume (1974) 167 is correct to point out that they may simply watch motionless as all eyes turn to the new entrant. No motivation is given for Demeas' appearance, and its striking manner would direct attention from such concerns; but it might be supposed that he leaves his house in

[18] For entrances with interrupted speech see on *Dysk.* 690.

exasperation with the distress of his household. The final lines of his monologue are fragmentary, but in all probability Demeas remains sufficiently absorbed in his anger to fail to notice the others until approached; see GS on 450–1.

520. *Exit* NIKERATOS *to his house*
In accordance with Demeas' request that he deny sanctuary to Chrysis (518), Nikeratos rushes indignantly off, perhaps pushing Moschion out of the way οὐ παρήϲειϲ; ('let me by, won't you?', 520) in a movement reminiscent of Demeas' treatment of the cook when he left earlier to drive out Chrysis (359–60), the first in a number of deliberate similarities between the two expulsions. During his absence from the stage, Moschion is able to convince his father of the true nature of what has happened.

532. *Enter* NIKERATOS *from his house*
Nikeratos enters in confusion, looking for Demeas (538): the door announcement (532) is cut short by his emotional entrance (cf. n. 18 above) and GS on 532–4 remark that the door noise is used to terminate the conversation on stage and focus attention on the new entrant.[19] Nikeratos' soliloquy of astonishment and distress contains a number of verbal echoes of Demeas' monologue prior to the scenes leading up to Chrysis' first expulsion (206 ff.) which are collected by Blundell (1980) 42.

539. *Exit* MOSCHION *to one side*
Nikeratos is observed and overheard by Demeas and Moschion as he enters and relates what he has seen within (532): Moschion, understandably reluctant to meet him now that he is on the verge of learning the truth about his violated daughter, delivers a clear exit-line and leaves in fear despite his father's encouragement (539). His direction of departure is unclear from the text both here and at his return in act v, beyond the fact that he does not enter Demeas' house (for he is later unaware of the wedding preparations: see GS on 538–41): Austin (1970) ad loc. suggests that he may leave for the city. Moschion's exit is necessary to enable the following scene between the two fathers to proceed unimpeded; so GS on 538–41. His departure before contact with Nikeratos is made possible by the latter's initial unawareness of being overheard, which prompts his almost verbatim repetition of his report to Demeas (535–6, 540–1): Nikeratos' words on entry are

[19] See for further examples B(2) above.

delivered as a soliloquy and warn Moschion to leave, enabling the old men to converse alone.

547. *Exit* NIKERATOS *to his house*
Nikeratos leaves in a rage to investigate further, rushing off without even completing his sentence: Demeas attempts to hold him back, but to no avail as is shown by the exit acknowledgement οἴχεται, ('he's gone'), which is something of a cry of despair.[20] In the following soliloquy Demeas interprets off-stage noises for the audience in terms similar to those used earlier by the cook to describe Demeas' own angry scene indoors (553, cf. 364).

556. *Enter* NIKERATOS *from his house*
Nikeratos' re-entrance is carefully prepared yet develops in an unexpected direction: Demeas' lengthy monologue expressing his certainty of imminent disaster and reporting on the threatening noises from within culminates in a door announcement where the choice of verb (555) reflects the violence of the action,[21] and in an impressive description of Nikeratos' fury (555–6). By analogy with the earlier scene of Demeas' rage (359–60) to which a number of clear allusions have been made,[22] the audience might expect Nikeratos to emerge driving Chrysis out before him: however, his actual appearance is a surprise as the old man unexpectedly enters alone frustrated by his household, and the anticipated expulsion is momentarily delayed. Nikeratos gives his motivation for re-entry at 563: he wants to tell Demeas of his plan before murdering Chrysis.

563. *Exit* NIKERATOS *to his house*
The action is now moving very quickly and accordingly Nikeratos dashes back inside without an explicit exit-line, leaving Demeas to deliver an exit acknowledgement εἰσπεπήδηκεν ('he's leapt inside', 564) which reflects the speed of his depature; compare 361 above and *Dysk.* 602.

568. *Enter* CHRYSIS *with the baby from* NIKERATOS' *house*
Demeas' door announcement (567) directs the audience's attention to Chrysis who rushes out in extreme distress which is expressed in her

[20] See C(5)(*b*) above.
[21] See B(2) above.
[22] Pushing someone out of the way when rushing inside (520, cf. 359–60); choice of phrase recalling that of Demeas (532f., cf. 206–7); monologue of character left on stage containing reference to off-stage noises (553, cf. 364) and identical door announcement (555, cf. 366–7).

elevated lament; on the tragic vocabulary see GS ad loc. In her heightened emotional state she fails to see Demeas and responds with surprise when he addresses her (569).

570. *Enter* NIKERATOS *from his house*
Nikeratos arrives in hot pursuit of Chrysis: Demeas appears to move between her and her pursuer since at 572a Nikeratos orders him to 'get out of the way', and the movement was presumably made as he addressed Chrysis and urged her to go indoors (569). She remains, however, probably still uncertain of Demeas following his furious treatment of her earlier.

575. *Exit* CHRYSIS *with the baby to* DEMEAS' *house*
Chrysis finally leaves, overcoming her initial mistrust which caused the instruction to be repeated twice (569, 574, 575) before it was finally obeyed: presumably she is eventually convinced of Demeas' good will towards her as he physically restrains Nikeratos from attacking her, and the old men struggle on-stage in an impressive scene.

Nikeratos states his intention to go and kill his wife at 580–1, but is delayed by Demeas: this delayed exit introduces the important following scene in which Nikeratos is outmanœuvred and made to calm down and agree to the marriage.[23]

614. *Exit* NIKERATOS *to his house*
Demeas has now succeeded in mollifying Nikeratos and urges him to leave to prepare for the wedding (612–13): he agrees and probably turns to go with πόει ('do so', 613), and Demeas calls the complimentary 614a after him to encourage him on his way.[24]

615. *Exit* DEMEAS *to his house*
Left alone, Demeas delivers a brief monologue to round off the act, a device for which Blundell (1980) 51 collects parallel examples. Following the fight and argument shown on stage, the tension of the act is reduced by means of the farcical scene of persuasion (on which see GS 611) and results in the peaceful parting of the old men before the act-break.

[23] See C(4) above.
[24] See C(3) above.

ΧΟΡΟΥ

616. *Enter* MOSCHION *from the side*

Moschion's entrance monologue, which is both lengthy and serious, creates a new twist in the plot at a point where there appeared to be no further obstacles to a universally desired marriage: he has become resentful of Demeas' suspicions of him (619–22) and declares his motivation—delayed, as often, until the end of the monologue[25]—to be the intention to frighten his father by appearing to have resolved on overseas mercenary service (634–6). His direction of entry is unclear; see on 539.

641. *Enter* PARMENON *from the side*

Moschion gives a visual announcement of the slave (639–40) and, although he remarks on his timely arrival,[26] does not approach him for seventeen lines. GS on 641 explain that in performance the audience's attention would be fixed on the new entrant so that the apparent illogicality of Moschion's silence would go unnoticed: it is worth noting that the visual announcement is a powerful means of transferring the spotlight, so to speak, on to the newly arrived Parmenon. The slave too enters with a monologue which gives his second thoughts over his treatment as his reason for returning: the speech is marked by indignation, in which he is too engrossed to notice Moschion. GS on 642 comment on his 'comically solemn' opening words; on the relationship of these two entrance monologues see Blundell (1980) 44. Parmenon's direction of entry is unclear; see on 324.

664. *Exit* PARMENON *to* DEMEAS' *house*

Moschion has to repeat his instruction to Parmenon before he is obeyed: εἴcιθι | εἴcω ('go inside', 658–9), βάδιζε ('get going', 661): the slave's natural curiosity delays his execution of the order, a characteristic already observed at 190–1; as in that earlier scene his questions are impatiently brushed aside with καὶ ταχύ ('and fast!', 660; cf. καὶ ταχέωc 193); see Blume (1974) 263. Eventually Moschion resorts to a threat of violence not uncommon in such heated exchanges, involving

[25] See on *Dysk.* 522.

[26] On the phrase εἰc δέοντα καιρόν see W. H. Race, *TAPhA* 111 (1981), n. 5: 'By the time of Menander [καιρόc] has almost completely lost the classical sense of appropriateness as is shown by the need to add a qualifying word.'

a strap (662): see *Dysk.* 502. As Parmenon leaves in bewilderment over his master's purpose, Moschion calls after him to speed him on his way (663b–4a); see on 614 above.

670. *Enter* PARMENON *from* DEMEAS' *house*
Moschion delivers a door announcement which both reflects his momentary anxiety over confronting his father and directs the audience's attention to the new arrival: he may himself turn round to face the door (so GS on 669). The carefully created expectation that Demeas will enter is defeated by the reappearance of Parmenon, who is not even bringing the cloak and sword. The change of metre marks (as often) a change of mood as the pace of the action quickens with the following succession of exits and entrances; see GS on 669 and Blume (1974) 266.

682. *Exit* PARMENON *to* DEMEAS' *house*
The slave, still failing to comprehend his master's behaviour, has to be persuaded to carry out his errand by actual violence rather than, as before, a mere threat (679): he lingers at the door in a last attempt to convince Moschion that his report of the wedding is correct (681) but leaves in the face of the young man's renewed anger, and 682a is ironically shouted after him; see GS on 681.

687. *Enter* PARMENON *from* DEMEAS' *house*
690. *Enter* DEMEAS *from his house*
Since the impression has been created that Demeas will not appear by means of Parmenon's return with the sword and cloak and the news that no-one inside has seen him, the old man's unannounced and unexpected arrival has considerable dramatic impact which outweighs the improbability of its convenient timing. Since the wedding preparations are well advanced, Demeas emerges looking for his son the bridegroom, and his motivation is expressed by ποῦ 'στί ('where is he?'), a phrase recurrent in such entrances.[27] Blume (1974) 271 may not be correct to suppose that Demeas enters speaking back to someone within since by analogy with similar passages 690b is more likely to be an expression of his thoughts (see on *DE* 102): εἰπέ μοι ('tell me') is a favourite phrase of Demeas (see Sandbach (1970) 122) which need not imply a specific addressee.

[27] See B(4) above.

694. *Exit* PARMENON *to* DEMEAS' *house*

Parmenon's departure, which is necessary under the constraints of the three-actor rule if Nikeratos is to join Demeas and Moschion on stage, comes with explicit motivation to bid farewell to those indoors, and an explicit exit-line (694). However, the notion that the slave is to accompany his young master is entirely new, and GS on 693–4 are probably correct to argue that Parmenon should be supposed to have deduced that Moschion is not serious, and intends by his action to embarrass him further. This could be made clear in performance and would turn this necessary removal of the third speaking actor into a movement of some comic significance in the scene.

713. *Enter* NIKERATOS *from his house*

Nikeratos' first words are presumably addressed to his wife: compare 421 where he also enters complaining of being nagged and explicitly addresses her as γύναι ('wife'). The motivation for his timely arrival, which removes the need for Moschion to reply to Demeas' reasoned argument (so GS on 713 ff.), is not made explicit; but 714 implies that as preparations are at the stage when the bridegroom should fetch his bride, he enters to find Moschion; the sudden and unannounced appearance of a new and potentially explosive element in the scene would in any case sufficiently grip the audience's attention to gloss over its exact cause. Nikeratos' attention is necessarily directed back into the house during 713–14, and he first becomes aware of the situation on stage at 715a where his astonished παῖ τί τοῦτο; ('whatever's this?') echoes the reaction of Demeas at 691a.

723. *Exit* NIKERATOS *to his house*

Nikeratos pauses only briefly for confirmation before complying with Demeas' instructions at 723.

725. *Enter* NIKERATOS *and his* DAUGHTER *from his house*

Who are witnesses of 726? GS ad loc. suggest they are 'members of the two households, played by supers'; Blume (1974) 282 appears to believe that the bride's mother and household slaves are meant. There are cogent reasons for rejecting these suggestions: witnesses were not legally necessary in Athens at a betrothal[28] but when present appear to have been invariably adult male citizens[29] and this, in addition to the severe legal disabilities regarding the role of women and slaves as

[28] See W. Erdmann, *Die Ehe im Alten Griechenland* (Munich, 1934), 242, 313.
[29] Cf. ibid. 242.

witnesses,[30] rules out the suggestions of GS and Blume. When a betrothal takes place in Menander, witnesses are sometimes used and sometimes not,[31] and accordingly the reference to witnesses here must have some point as it might otherwise easily have been omitted. Demeas alone cannot be meant, as the reference is plural. It may be worth considering whether the reference is to the audience itself, now included in the action, so to speak, as it had been earlier at 487–8 where Demeas questioned his son ἐναντίον | . . . τῶν παρόντων ('before those present') which both GS ad loc. and Bain (1977) 170 n. 1 take to refer to the audience. If so, the spectators are given a participatory role in the final unravelling of the plot, which Nikeratos would perhaps in performance clarify by a gesture.

730. *Enter* CHRYSIS *from* DEMEAS' *house*

The suggestion of Austin(1970) ad loc. that Demeas calls through the door to Chrysis who then enters is more likely than supposing her to enter with Demeas at 690 (cf. GS on 729), as no reference is made to her until now, and her silent presence would only distract from the confrontation of Moschion and his father (694 ff.).

732. *Enter* MUTE SLAVE *from* DEMEAS' *house*

In response to Demeas' summons a mute enters with a torch and garlands (cf. on *Dysk.* 964a): unusually for a mute, he is given a visual announcement.[32]

737. *Exeunt omnes to* DEMEAS' *house*

As Demeas speaks the final lines (a variation on the apparently traditional formula; see on *Dysk.* 969), a wedding procession forms (συμπροπέμπωμεν 'escort in procession', 732a) and at the end departs to be received and conducted inside by Chrysis in a scene which gives a visible attainment to the marriage which has been repeatedly thwarted in the play (cf. Blume (1974) 284–5).

[30] See A. R. W. Harrison, *The Law of Athens*, ii (Oxford, 1971), 136–7, 147 ff.

[31] With witnesses: *Aspis* 504–1. Without witnesses: *Dysk.* 842; *Mis.* 444; *Perik.* 1013; *Fab. Inc.* 29. At *Dysk.* 762 Gorgias calls the gods to witness.

[32] On mutes generally see A(2) above.

10

Sikyonios

[*Enter* PROLOGUE-SPEAKER]

The detailed account of the background to the plot given in the first part of the opening fragments gives the impression that these lines come from a prologue, an impression confirmed by the apparently verbatim repetition at 23–4 of the formula found at *Dysk.* 45–6 at the close of Pan's prologue. Much, however, is unclear, not least the identity of the speaker beyond his or her probable divinity, which can be deduced from the display of knowledge (cf. GS on 1–24): H. Lloyd-Jones[1] suggests Demeter or a minor divinity of the Eleusinian cult, while Webster (1974) 182, pointing out the importance of the examination of credentials in the play, favours a personified Elenchos, citing fr. 717 K.-T. Whether the prologue was initial or delayed cannot be deduced from the fragments, and comparison with the initial prologue of *Dysk.* is of doubtful value despite the repeated lines, as there is no reason to suppose Menander to have aimed at any further similarities between the two speeches.

[*Exit* PROLOGUE-SPEAKER]

The point at which the prologue ends and the following conversation begins is uncertain. The last line which clearly belongs to the prologue is 24 (from the apparently formulaic audience-address), but Merkelbach[2] compares the visual announcement which follows with the formula in *Dysk.* 47–8 and suggests that οὑτοςί ('this man here', 29) may be among the last words of the prologue-speaker as he or she announces the new arrivals; compare τουτονί at *Dysk.* 47.

[*Enter a* WOMAN *and her* DIALOGUE PARTNER]

That one of the speakers in the following scene is a woman is guaranteed by the characteristically female turns of phrase (on which see GS on 25–35) but further details of her or her dialogue partner are not available.

The action of the lost section until 110 towards the end of act iii is

[1] *GRBS* 7 (1966), 155.
[2] *MH* 23 (1966), 173 n. 7.

almost completely irrecoverable: the fragmentary lines 36–109 give no firm clues to the identity of the speakers or the circumstances of their delivery. Webster (1974) 183 collects possible inferences on the events of this gap from the more preserved portions of the play, and GS on 52–109 discuss some interpretations of the surviving lines.

125. *Enter* PYRRHIAS *from the side*[3]
When the text resumes, Theron and Stratophanes are on stage engaged in dialogue. The visual announcement of Pyrrhias appears to begin in the now lost opening of 120: possible supplements are collected by Kassel (1965) ad loc. and by GS on 119–20, none of which seems clearly preferable to the others. The announcement begins six lines before contact is made, which allows the new arrival to be identified to the audience by name, suggesting that this may be his first appearance, and enables Stratophanes to outline the mission on which the slave has been sent (122–3). As often with visual announcements,[4] a description of the entrant's apparent mood deduced from his manner prepares the audience for the effect of his news (124); Kassel (1965) ad loc. lists a number of parallels. The resulting lengthy and detailed introduction signals the importance of Pyrrhias' arrival and of his report, which he is able to deliver as soon as contact is made, with no delay for greetings or explanation.

149. *Exeunt* STRATOPHANES, THERON, *and* PYRRHIAS *to the side*[5]
Stratophanes issues the order to depart at 145b, having read the letter while Theron delivers an aside (144–5a): as GS comment on 144, as a soldier Stratophanes is accustomed to giving orders. Theron's two attempts at delay in the hope of hearing the news in more detail (146b, 147a) are firmly overruled by Stratophanes who repeats his orders[6] and leads the group off. Not only does this interplay illustrate the characters and relationship of Stratophanes and his parasite (so GS on 146),[7] but it also provides an intriguing ending to the act, as the soldier's intended course of action is concealed from the audience.

[3] The slave returns from visiting Stratophanes' supposed mother in Sikyon, but as the setting of the play is unclear (see GS, pp. 632–3) his direction of entry is equally irrecoverable.

[4] See B(1) in the first part of this book.

[5] As emerges from the following act, the group leaves to Eleusis, but on which side of the stage this lay is unclear; cf. n. 3 above.

[6] On the text see E. W. Handley, *BICS* 26 (1979), 83.

[7] On delayed exits for characterization see C(4) above.

ΧΟΡΟΥ

150. *Enter* TWO CHARACTERS, *presumably from the side*[8]

Two characters enter in mid-conversation as the first derides the opinion held by the second that a man has a good cause simply because he puts up an emotional display, and the implication is that this has been their topic of conversation prior to entry. Despite the plurals at 172 and 175 there is no firm evidence of the presence of a third character in this scene; GS 647 compare the plurals at *Dysk.* 455, 562. However, beyond the fact that the first speaker is said to have oligarchic sympathies which the second speaker does not share (156), and that the subject of their discussion is apparently Stratophanes' actions at Eleusis (cf. GS on 150ff.), this opening scene is beset with obscurities. Clues to the identities of the speakers are unreliable: at 156 the letters cμ̣[are preserved, which may imply 'Smikrines' but also 'Smikrion' or 'Smikrias'; see GS ad loc. The second speaker is unnamed in the fragmentary lines up to his departure at 168.

168. *Exit* SECOND SPEAKER *to the side*

The conversation, which has been acrimonious from the start, deteriorates into an exchange of insults, and most probably the second speaker leaves the stage and 'Smikrines' vaunts over him, apparently victorious in the exchange, with οἴμωζε ('go to hell!', 167: cf. *Epitr.* 376; *Sam.* 294). Although this insult provokes a response, 'Smikrines'' following words (167b–168) are addressed with impunity to the other's departing back.[9] Quite why the second speaker leaves is irrecoverable from the lacunose text, and his direction of exit is also unclear beyond the fact that if, as seems likely, he leaves by one of the side entrances, it will not be towards Eleusis, from which direction the messenger enters at 169.

169. *Enter* MESSENGER *from Eleusis*

The strongest reason for supposing the speaker of 169 to be a new entrant is the clear contrast of style between the derisive dismissal implied by 167–8 and the elevated expression of 169, the call which delays 'Smikrines' on stage and introduces a scene with a number of elements from tragedy: on the tragic style see Sandbach (1970) 128–9,

[8] Presumably they enter from Eleusis having heard some report of the events there, but this is uncertain.

[9] On this device see C(3) above.

GS on 169. On this view the Messenger[10] calls to 'Smikrines' who appears to be moving to enter his house after the departure of his original dialogue partner, and the resulting delayed exit introduces, as often, an important scene, and contributes to the tragic effect.[11] GS on 150ff. and 169 are unconvinced that the Messenger is not the same person as the original dialogue partner of 'Smikrines', pointing out that at 172 and 175 'Smikrines' assumes his addressee can report on the meeting, an odd assumption if he had only appeared at 169: Sandbach (1970) 130 also remarks on the difficulty of assigning any significance to the opening scene of the act if the first dialogue partner leaves at 168. However, these problems may both stem from obscurities of the plot caused by the loss of many of the earlier scenes, and cannot be taken as fatal objections to the appearance of a new character at 169.

271. *Exeunt severally, the* MESSENGER *to one side,* 'SMIKRINES' *to his house* The following scene has been much debated, and as yet no wholly satisfying solution has been proposed. The most likely restoration of the papyrus at 271, ἀλλ' ἀπέ[ρχομαι ('but I'm off!'; cf. West's restoration at *Sam.* 162), produces an explicit exit announcement which makes the messenger's departure unavoidable, and which may be a verbal echo of the ending of the Messenger-speech in Euripides' *Orestes*, to which allusions have already been made; so GS ad loc. Presumably the Messenger leaves by the side opposite from his point of entry, as there is no sign that he meets the new arrivals from Eleusis at 272.

The most convincing explanation of the following action has been put forward by Sandbach,[12] whose arguments need no detailed repetition: he supposes both the Messenger and 'Smikrines' to leave, and that Stratophanes now enters, followed by Moschion who, defeated at the meeting, is making a last attempt to strike back at his rival. The difficulty of this proposal, as Sandbach himself acknowledges,[13] comes in the deployment of actors under the three-actor rule,

[10] The scribe's βλεπηιϲ (188) is perhaps less likely to represent a proper name than a parenthetic question as suggested by Chantraine: —βλέπειϲ;—. Cf. parenthetic μανθάνειϲ *Perik.* 338 and *Sam.* 378; ὁρᾶιϲ *Perik.* 332. See also F. W. Handley, *BICS* 12 (1965), 49–50.

[11] On delayed exits generally see C(4) above, and on the tragic effect of the abrupt appearance and departure cf. Sandbach (1970) 129.

[12] *PCPhS* 12 (1967), 41ff.

[13] Ibid. 43–4.

which if applied here would involve two speaking actors departing in different directions at 271, one of whom must in the very next line re-enter with the third speaking actor in a new scene, apparently having had no time to change costume and move from either the opposite wing or the *skene*-building to make an entrance from the wing leading from Eleusis. The problem is formidable, and invites a variety of responses. Webster[14] rejects Sandbach's staging and prefers to continue the dialogue between the Messenger and 'Smikrines', but does not explain why a charge of kidnapping is suddenly made or indeed by whom. Sandbach (1975) 197 n. 1 defends both his proposed staging and his belief in the three-actor rule by suggesting a slow and silent withdrawal by 'Smikrines' on the Messenger's departure, which would allow time for the costume-change. This would however be unparalleled in extant Menander, where such necessary intervals are elsewhere covered by, for example, brief monologues:[15] here a few lines delivered by 'Smikrines' in reaction to the Messenger's report could if needed easily cover the time required for a costume-change, but this Menander has chosen not to do. The most extreme solution would be to take this passage as decisive evidence against the existence of a three-actor rule in Menander, as it appears to need four speaking actors. However, it would be rash to allow one puzzling and disputed scene whose contents, participants, and action are so unclear, and which swiftly becomes hopelessly fragmentary, to outweigh the evidence in favour of the rule.[16] At present the staging of 271–2 remains uncertain, and even Sandbach's explanation, which accounts for most of the issues raised by the contents of the lines, poses problems which are as yet unresolved.

272. *Enter* STRATOPHANES *and* PYRRHIAS *with* MOSCHION *in hot pursuit, from Eleusis*

The characters enter apparently in mid-dialogue, as Moschion issues a threat to Stratophanes and his slave (ἡμᾶϲ in 273a strongly supports Austin's supplement ὑμᾶϲ in 272), an aggressive arrival which stands in marked contrast to the previous lengthy narrative and silent withdrawal of 'Smikrines' (see above). GS on 272ff. suppose Theron to accompany Stratophanes, but this is open to doubt: if the parasite does enter here, he must leave at some point before the choral

[14] *Studies in Later Greek Comedy*² (Manchester, 1970), 187.
[15] See A(1) above.
[16] See A(1) above.

interlude on the mission in fulfilment of which he returns with Kichesias in act v, but it is unclear there whether Stratophanes had sent him originally with instructions to fetch a false witness or whether he had devised the plan of his own accord, in which case he need not appear with Stratophanes here at the end of act iv. The evidence is ambiguous: on the one hand it is hard to imagine how a scene of Stratophanes instructing Theron to fetch a false witness would fit into the emotional recognition scenes which apparently follow swiftly after 272ff.; but on the other hand, one of the many unexplained details of these fragmentary scenes is Theron's awareness of Stratophanes' whereabouts in 'Smikrines' house at 365, an odd piece of knowledge had he not witnessed at least part of the recognition scene in act iv. Judgement on Theron's whereabouts at 272 is then best left suspended, but a likely attendant for Stratophanes is Pyrrhias his slave (cf. 145–9) whose presence would provoke the plurals ὑμᾶϲ and ἡμᾶϲ (272–3).

[*Exit* MOSCHION *to* 'SMIKRINES' *house*]
[*Enter* 'SMIKRINES' *and* WIFE *from his house*]

311. *Exeunt* 'SMIKRINES', *his* WIFE, STRATOPHANES, *and* PYRRHIAS *to* 'SMIKRINES' *house*

The text up to 305 is too fragmentary to allow any useful conclusions to be drawn concerning the movements of the characters beyond the general conjectures made above, on which see GS on 280ff. On completion of the recognition scene they all leave into 'Smikrines' ' house, from which Stratophanes next appears, talking back to his mother (377); their motivation may be to find Moschion. The gap in 310 may have contained an explicit exit instruction issued by 'Smikrines', a movement apparently prepared in 305.

ΧΟΡΟΥ

312. *Enter* KICHESIAS *and* THERON *from the side*

The two characters enter in mid-conversation to begin a scene whose nature can be deduced, despite its fragmentary state, from comparison with Plautus' *Poenulus*.[17] In presenting the entrance and faced with the requirement to delay the scene of Theron's proposition to Kichesias until the couple appear before the audience, Menander has succeeded

[17] Cf. GS on 343ff.; A. S. Gratwick, in E. J. Kennedy, ed., *The Cambridge History of Classical Literature*, ii (Cambridge, 1982), 101–3.

in providing a plausible reason for the old man to follow the parasite from, presumably, the city: Kichesias enters complaining about the long walk and Theron's refusal to give details of why he wants him. Entry in mid-conversation is a common enough device in Menander when two people enter together,[18] but here, as GS comment on 312, it is used to create a supremely natural effect since it may be supposed that Theron has a positive reason for the delay, namely, his wish to build some relationship with Kichesias before making his suggestion.

361. *Enter* DROMON *from Eleusis*

Although Dromon's opening speech is largely fragmentary, the careful construction of the wholly preserved first line (see GS ad loc.) suggests that this is an entrance monologue rather than the beginning of an address by the slave to his old master following a period of eavesdropping, as Kassel (1965) ad loc. supposed; see Bain (1977) 204–5. The entrance monologue is delivered initially in unawareness of the couple on stage who themselves fail to observe the new arrival, Kichesias being engrossed in emotional memories (359–60a), Theron in admiration for what he supposes to be his companion's acting-ability (360b). Presumably Dromon's speech gave his motivation for entry, having fulfilled his mission at Eleusis (cf. 266–70), and π]α̣τ̣ε̣ρ̣ ('her father', 362) marks his observation of Kichesias.

367. *Exit* THERON *to* 'SMIKRINES'' *house*

When Kichesias faints (363; cf. *Aspis* 299) Dromon sends Theron for water, an order the parasite acknowledges and supplements by promising to send Stratophanes out: however, Kichesias' swift revival removes the need for water and accordingly Theron need not reappear from the house, which allows the third speaking actor to change and re-emerge as the soldier.[19] The swift bustle which results creates a slapstick and comic element which relieves the tension of Kichesias' collapse.

377. *Enter* STRATOPHANES *from* 'SMIKRINES'' *house*

Stratophanes, summoned by Theron (363–4), enters talking back to his mother within, which may be intended to show that his parents are aware of events (so GS on 377).

[18] See B(6) above.

[19] On Theron's failure to reappear despite his characteristic curiosity see F. H. Sandbach, *The Comic Theatre of Greece and Rome* (London, 1977), 79–80.

385. *Exeunt* DROMON *and* KICHESIAS *to Eleusis*
Kichesias is plainly overwhelmed by events, as his small share in the dialogue shows: Dromon however is eager to go, as his repeated encouragement shows (note the fragmentary verbs in]ωμεν at 382 and 385) and he leads his master off in accordance with Stratophanes' instructions (383). Naturally, they leave to find Philoumene at Eleusis, and the lacunose 382 probably contained an explicit statement of their destination.

386. *Enter* DONAX *from* STRATOPHANES' *house*

396. *Exeunt* DONAX *to* STRATOPHANES' *house, and* STRATOPHANES *to Eleusis*
The mute Donax departs with his orders (385, 395) and Stratophanes leaves to follow Kichesias and Dromon in fulfilment of his promise of 383–4: the length of his speech serves no obvious dramatic purpose but may, as GS on 386ff. suggest, have been necessary to allow one of the speaking actors who have just left to change costume to play the young man in the following scene.[20]

397. *Enter* MOSCHION *from* 'SMIKRINES'' *house*
Moschion's entrance monologue, in which he regretfully abandons his hopes of Philoumene, is both lengthy and sad (cf. the examination by Blundell (1980) 67) and so stands in marked contrast to the bustling and optimistic scenes which come before: his appearance allows the audience to view what has happened from a quite different angle. In the extant fragments Moschion gives no specific reason for his entrance, but one may have been provided in the lost sections, perhaps deliberately held back until the end; cf. on *Dysk.* 522. It is clear from Stratophanes' appearance at 377 that those indoors are aware of the new developments.

423. *Exeunt omnes*
The characters leave to celebrate the wedding which must have been arranged between Stratophanes and Philoumene, although beyond this the plot of the closing scenes is quite uncertain. Traditional elements at the conclusion of the play are torches and garlands (418–19), an appeal for applause (420–1), and the invocation of Victory (421–2) which is contained in lines repeated in other Menandrean comedies; see on *Dysk.* 969.

[20] On the three-actor rule see A(1) above.

Index